THE TOPOGRAPHY AND LAYOUT OF MEDIEVAL DROGHEDA

GW00671703

JOHN BRADLEY

PUBLISHED BY THE OLD DROGHEDA SOCIETY
PRINTED BY NORTH EAST PRINTERS LTD. 1997

(Reprinted by permission of the County Louth Archaeological & Historical Society)

Acknowledgements

The Old Drogheda Society wishes to acknowledge the following for their assistance in this publication

- The County Louth Archaeological and Historical Society for permission to reprint this article from their Journal Vol. XIX, No.2, 1978.
- The Corporation of Drogheda for both part-funding this publication and permission to reproduce the two Ricciardelli paintings and that of Bathe House.
- Drogheda Partnership for part-funding this publication.
- Mrs. Nesbit Waddington for granting permission to reproduce the Van der Hagen painting of Drogheda.
- The National Gallery in respect of the Place sketch of St. Sundays Gate.

List of Figures

List of Plates

Preface to the 1997 Edition

This study of medieval Drogheda was written almost twenty years ago. It arose out of a fortunate combination of circumstances. I had just completed a thesis on the topography of medieval Irish towns and I was working under the direction of Professor George Eogan on the archaeological excavations at Knowth, Co. Meath. The excavation team was based at Townley Hall where we had access to Professor Frank Mitchell's notable library which included several publications on Drogheda and an excellent run of the *County Louth Archaeological and Historical Journal*. My nascent interest in Drogheda was encouraged and developed by Moira Corcoran and Noel Ross, and with the older publications readily to hand it was an enjoyable, albeit time-consuming, labour to extract the references and try to make sense of them. By and large, the study has withstood the test of time and I am honoured that the Old Drogheda Society has thought it worthy of reproduction. Inevitably, as a result of research during the intervening years, parts of the text need to be updated. Rather than make alterations, however, I have chosen to refer the reader to the major publications which have appeared since.

The 1970s was a period of great physical change in Drogheda and much of its ancient building fabric was lost. My study was prompted by the demolition of John Street in 1976, a process of dismantling and bulldozing which was carried out without archaeological or architectural recording of any kind. Accordingly, a major conclusion of this study was that, in future, archaeological work should take place in advance of redevelopment. At the time it was by no means clear that such work would take place but in the intervening years Drogheda has witnessed a great deal of archaeological excavation and the results of some of this work have already appeared in print notably the papers by David Sweetman, "Archaeological excavations at Shop Street, Drogheda, Co. Louth" in *Proceedings of the Royal Irish Academy* 84 C (1984), pp. 171-224; Kieran Campbell, "A medieval tile kiln site at Magdalene Street, Drogheda" in *County Louth Archaeological and Historical Journal* 21, no. 1 (1985), pp. 48-54; Andrew Halpin and Laureen Buckley, "Archaeological excavations at the Dominican Priory, Drogheda, Co. Louth", *Proceedings of the Royal Irish Academy* 95 C (1995), pp. 175-253; and Eoin Halpin, "Excavations at St Mary d'Urso, Drogheda, Co. Louth" in *County Louth Archaeological and Historical Journal* 23, no. 4 (1996).

Other archaeological features have been the subject of study by Kieran Campbell, "Some medieval floor tiles from Drogheda", *Journal of the Old Drogheda Society*, No. 5 (1986), pp. 14-20: and Heather A. King, "A possible market cross fragment from Drogheda", *County Louth Archaeological and Historical Journal* 20, no. 4 (1984), pp. 334-339: while the paper by G. F. Mitchell and C. A. Dickson, "Plant remains and other items from medieval Drogheda", *Circaea* 3, no. 1 (1985), pp. 31-37, demonstrates how environmental evidence can provide an insight into the diet and craft activities that were practiced in medieval times. In addition Kieran Campbell has published a useful overview, "The archaeology of medieval Drogheda", *Archaeology Ireland* 1 (1987), pp. 52-56, while V. M. Buckley and P. D. Sweetman, *Archaeological Survey of County Louth* (Dublin 1991) provides detailed descriptions of all surviving medieval monuments in Drogheda.

Several medieval documentary sources containing material of relevance to Drogheda have been published in *Analecta Hibernica* and *Archivium Hibernicum*. In particular one may note Elizabeth Dowse and Margaret Murphy, "Rotulus clausus de anno 48 Edward III - a reconstruction", *Analecta Hibernica* 35 (1992), pp. 87-154; Anthony Lynch, "Religion in late medieval Ireland", *Archivium Hibernicum* 36 (1981), pp. 3-15 and the same author's "Five documents of Drogheda interest from the registers of the archbishop of Armagh", *County Louth Archaeological and Historical Journal* 21, no. 4 (1988), pp. 407-414.

Information of value is also to be found in G. O. Sayles (ed.) *Documents on the affairs of Ireland before king's council* (Dublin 1979); G. MacNiocaill (ed.) *Crown surveys of lands* 1540-41 *with the Kildare Rental begun in 1518* (Dublin 1992); and in Brendan Smith (ed.), *The register of Milo Sweteman, Archbishop of Armagh* 1361-1380 (Dublin 1997). Much work still remains to be done, however, on the political and economic history of Drogheda during the later middle ages but several insights on the town's political roles are to be found in Susan O'Connor's study "Tudor Drogheda", *Journal of the Old Drogheda Society*, No. 10 (1996) pp. 86-111. The overseas trade of medieval Drogheda has been placed in its wider context by Timothy O'Neill, *Merchants and Mariners in Medieval Ireland* (Dublin 1987) and by Wendy Childs and Timothy O'Neill, in their chapter on "Overseas trade" in A. Cosgrove (ed) A *new history of Ireland*, vol. 2 (Oxford 1987), pp. 492-524.

In 1984 I had the opportunity of re-examining much of the material published here when I was commissioned by the Office of Public Works to prepare an *Urban Archaeology Survey of County Louth*. The report was concerned primarily with describing the standing remains of medieval date within Drogheda and documenting those which had vanished. The main topographical result was that a re-examination of Francis Place's *Views* of c.1698 and Ravell's map of 1749 (reprinted by the County Louth Archaeological and Historical Society in 1991), convinced me that the town wall had continued along the river bank on both sides of the Boyne and that several mural towers and turrets had been built along the river front, a conclusion that Avril Thomas also arrived at in her useful study *Walled Towns in Ireland* (1992). The Urban Archaeology Survey report on Drogheda has not been published but it may be consulted in the archive of the National Monuments & Historic Properties Service, Department of Arts, Heritage, the Gaeltacht and the Islands, 51 St Stephen's Green Dublin 2.

Architectural features within the town have been the subject of study by William Garner, *Drogheda Architectural Heritage* (Dublin 1986) in which he has identified a handful of surviving half-timbered buildings. Other architectural surveys include Nicholas Sheaf, "Northern garrison of the Pale--Drogheda, Co. Louth", *Country Life* (July 1980), pp. 186-188, 299-303 and the section on Drogheda in Christine Casey and Alastair Rowan, *The Buildings of Ireland: North Leinster* (Harmonsworth 1993). Other useful studies include Tom Reilly, *Tracing Drogheda's medieval walls* (Drogheda 1995), James Garry, *The Streets and Lanes of Drogheda* (Drogheda 1996) and Patrick Duffner, *The Low Lane Church* 1300-1979: *the story of the Augustinians in Drogheda* (Drogheda 1979). Mention must also be made of the *Journal of the Old Drogheda Society* which, commencing with volume 1 in 1976, has provided an important forum for the publication of local research.

Finally, it remains for me to thank the County Louth Archaeological and Historical Society for publishing the original article and for generously granting permission to reprint it.

John Bradley.

Department of Modern History,
National University of Ireland,
Maynooth.
October, 1997

THE TOPOGRAPHY AND LAYOUT OF MEDIEVAL DROGHEDA

By John Bradley

Two hundred years ago when the Neapolitan artist Gabriele Ricciardelli visited Drogheda it was still largely untouched by the Industrial Revolution. His paintings convey the calmness of a rural atmosphere in a stable commercial setting.[1] The south side of the Boyne was dominated then by the tall late medieval tower of St. Mary's Parish Church while the Millmount had already begun to function as a military barracks. A single bridge of three arches crossed the river, to the east of which ships were drawn up beside the docks. The north side of the town was the larger and the houses were built more closely together than on the south. Most of the houses were slated but some had thatched roofs. Shop Street was lined with red brick buildings, three and four storeys high. The public buildings - the Tholsel, St. Peter's Church, the Grammar School - were prominent structures. The town's most striking feature however, was the degree to which portions of the medieval fabric survived. The circuit of the town walls was almost completely intact and indeed still delimited the town's extent. Massive medieval gatehouses stood at the ends of West Street, Fair Street and Laurence Street. The river wall was almost complete along the north side and four mural towers remained on the north wall which still had its original arcading. The ruined towers and remains of the parish church of St. Mary, the hospital of St. Mary d'Urso, the Dominican friary and the hospital of St. John the Baptist were present. It was a picture not much different from that which Place drew in 1698.

Most of the medieval fabric which Ricciardelli saw is now gone and in attempting to visualise what medieval Drogheda looked like, sources other than the surviving buildings alone must be utilised. Even then the picture that emerges does not form a coherent pattern but is rather a spatter of images. Documentary sources for Drogheda, as for most Irish towns, are slight until the sixteenth century. This means that the archaeological record is the one with most potential for understanding the period before 1500. No archaeological excavation has yet taken place in Drogheda but some inferences can be drawn from stray finds. It is clear from the recent mechanical digging in John Street, which destroyed evidence relating to medieval tenements and the town defences, that the town is particularly rich in archaeological material. It is to be hoped that when other archaeologically important areas of the town are being redeveloped proper investigation will take place. It cannot be emphasised too much that because our knowledge of Drogheda's origins and early growth is so slight, the destruction of archaeological deposits there is inexcusable. In this paper, in which I have tried to examine the early layout of Drogheda, I wish to point out the extent to which the town's past survives *beneath, on* as well as *above* the ground. Further I have attempted to put together all relevant topographical details in order to form the background on which archaeological research can build.

The Sources

The sources for the study of medieval Drogheda may be regarded as documentary, archaeological and topographical. The documentary sources tend to be incidental and no medieval civic records survive. What can be inferred of civic life from the documents is therefore selective. The origin of many of these documents is ecclesiastical. The *Registers of the Armagh Primates* contain information relating to trials, synods and visitations, but also have occasional references to church furnishings and domestic equipment, and to houses and citizens of the town.[2] Monasteries and churches held land within the town and the details of many properties are to be found in their registers and cartularies.[3] The details of tenements held by private individuals survive in some cases. The *Gormanston Register* contains the leases of sixty two properties bought up by the Prestons between 1307 and 1374.[4] The *Dowdall Deeds* contain two wills, one tenement deed and a few isolated references to holdings and streets.[5] The royal administrative records, the statutes of the Irish Parliament and the Ormond deeds provide evidence for the town's internal organisation, trading connection and political status.[6] The principal town charters have been gathered together by MacNiocaill.[7] Two fragmentary Drogheda chronicles dating to the seventeenth century, but drawing on earlier sources, are known.[8]

Documents of the seventeenth and later centuries are of use in identifying forgotten buildings and street names. The *Council Book of Drogheda Corporation*, title deeds, rentals, letters and journals contain information which may be used to pinpoint the location of churches and private houses as well as helping to envisage the original appearance of structures which have been demolished since.[9]

Many of the secondary sources are worthwhile. D'Alton's *History of Drogheda*, published in 1844, is one of the better urban histories of its time and is still unsurpassed as a narrative account.[10] Papers by Allen, Matthew Kelly, Maurice Sheehy and Moira Corcoran have examined specific features of the medieval town.[11] The drawback of these works however is that no attempt has been made to trace the town's topographical development as a whole, or to produce maps showing stages in its development.

The early maps of Drogheda are extremely important in examining the town's growth and the survival of archaic features. It is very fortunate that a sixteenth century plan survives as it gives a picture of what Drogheda was like at the end of the medieval period.[12] The map like other sixteenth century plans, must be used with caution. Barnaby Goche, its author, was not a skilled map maker and when his Drogheda map is compared with the works of Speed's cartographers it appears to be nothing more than a sketch. Yet even Speed's methods were notoriously rough and ready; his map of Bristol (c. 1610) took two days to complete, while at Southampton the same cartographer reconstructed a castle known to have been in ruin in his own day.[13] Avril Thomas has pointed out that the variation in detail in Goche's map may reflect his knowledge of the town. It follows therefore that Goche may only be regarded as reliable for what he puts in and little or no inferences can be made from his omissions. On the south side of the Boyne, Goche shows the concentration of houses to be along John Street, the Quays and Pitcher Hill. James's Street is not shown. On the north side he shows the settled area as being along the axes of Shop Street, Peter Street, Laurence Street, West Street and the Quays. Fair Street, William Street and all north-south linking streets are absent. It would be wrong to think that these streets did not exist, as from documentary records streets such as Fair Street can be seen to have been present from at least the fourteenth century. As Thomas has herself shown, the relationship of the buildings, walls and streets is also haphazard. Goche's map should not be accounted as anything more than an impression of the town in 1574. While it may be that Drogheda had declined considerably in extent and housing density by the close of the sixteenth century, Goche cannot be regarded as clear evidence for it.[14] The other important maps include Newcomen's of 1657, one of 1744, and Ravell's of 1749.[15] The first Ordnance Survey plan was prepared in 1835.

Since the late seventeenth century Drogheda has been frequented by artists and antiquaries, many of whom made paintings and drawings which are now important in examining the past appearance of the town. Individual buildings, such as the barbican of St. Laurence's Gate have received much attention.[16]

The archaeological sources may be divided into two groups, monuments and small finds. The surviving medieval monuments are the Millmount motte, portion of St. Mary's church, the tower of the Dominican friary and hospital, the church of the hospital of St. Mary d'Urso, the church of the hospital of St. Laurence known as the Cord church, and portions of the town wall at Millmount, St. Mary's Church, beside St. Laurence's Gate, near the West Gate, and also the barbican of St. Laurence's Gate and the arch of the Butter Gate.[17] Some carved stones from the medieval church of St. Peter survive.[18] The churchyard of St. Peter's contains the remains of seven sixteenth century tomb slabs.[19] A line impressed tile, probably of early fourteenth century date, and a Limoges medallion were found in the course of grave digging and are now on display inside the church.[20] The medallion is a circular copper disc with four perforations. On it is a representation of Christ with his right arm raised in blessing and his left clasping a book. It is most likely of thirteenth century date and would originally have formed part of a reliquary or book cover. Floor tiles have also been uncovered near the Dominican Friary and portion of the cemetery has come to light.[21] Two medieval fonts are known.[22] An armorial stone was found during trench laying in Shop Street.[23] During construction of the new ring road a medieval graveslab bearing a finely carved cross and shears, indicating that it was a memorial to a tailor, was found near the west end of West Street. It may have been connected with the church of St. Mary d'Urso; it is now in the Millmount museum. In the British Museum there are nine objects, acquired between 1854 and 1868 whose provenance is given as Drogheda.[24] The Blackmore museum, Salisbury, possesses two bronze axeheads which are listed as from Drogheda.[25] The whereabouts of the coin hoard of 1846, described as having been found "at Drogheda"[26] is unknown. Its precise find spot is equally uncertain although it would seem to have been found in a railway cutting. Only four coins were examined by the numismatist Aquilla Smith who identified them as three Kufic *dirhams* and one 'Cunnetti' penny from Viking York.[27] Prof. Dolley has suggested that on this evidence the hoard probably belonged to the first half of the tenth century.[28] In the summer of 1976 large quantities of medieval pottery were recovered during trench digging at John Street. Over 1000 sherds were found and these included a wide variety of imported wares as well as pottery of local manufacture. Most of it dated to the thirteenth and early fourteenth centuries. French pottery, both Saintonge and polychrome ware, and English pottery from Chester, Bristol, the north-west of England and possibly Gloucester were represented.[29]

The topographical sources may be regarded as the siting of the town, the internal arrangement of streets, buildings and street blocks, and placenames, which I propose to examine in more detail.

The Background

From the late twelfth until the early fourteenth centuries towns were established all over Europe in large numbers. The reasons for their appearance and growth, while unclear, are keenly debated.[30] The increase in population, the expansion of trade, the desire of the merchants for security and independent government, have been suggested. Whatever the reasons, the facts are plain. New lands were sought out and old ones conquered in a wave of settlement development. In Russia a host of new towns made their appearance along the riverine chains of the Dniepr and Dnestr; in the Rhineland and in Gascony tracts of forest land were cleared and planted with towns; in Devon and Cornwall the wasteland of the moors was settled; along the coast of Belgium and Holland new land was reclaimed from the sea; on the Baltic and in north Germany the Hanseatic League emerged; in the Mediterranean the waves of crusader activity generated towns such as Aigues-Mortes. In eastern Germany Slav lands were conquered and settled; in Spain the *reconquista* made land available; in north Wales garrison towns were set up in an effort to control the Welsh.[31] In Ireland, as in eastern Germany and Spain, old lands were conquered and large numbers of colonists were brought in, not just to keep the lands militarily stable, but to exploit and develop the country's resources and in the process to found towns.

Almost all the towns built in Ireland between 1180 and 1300 were Norman creations. The initial impact of Norman society on Ireland is conventionally dated to 1169 but there are many examples of earlier contact, particularly in Romanesque architecture and in a number of the Cistercian monasteries. The military contact began in May 1169 with the arrival of three ship-loads of mercenaries at Bannow Bay, Co. Wexford. Further contingents arrived in 1170 and assisted Diarmait

MacMurchada to regain his kingship of Leinster. On Diarmait's death Richard FitzGilbert de Clare, leader of the mercenaries, was acknowledged as the new king. The growth of the mercenaries' power threatened an independent Norman kingdom in Ireland and this most likely induced Henry II to cross from England in 1171 with an army of 4000 men with which to ensure his recognition as overlord of Ireland. Richard de Clare was acknowledged lord of Leinster, but the granting of Meath (comprising the present-day counties of Meath and Westmeath) to Hugh de Lacy in 1172 started a new phase of conquest and colonisation. It is probable that the colonisation of Leinster started almost immediately after Henry II left Ireland. The founding of Dunbrody Abbey (1173) marks the beginning of new church organisation within the Norman areas and by 1176, when de Clare died, the process of colonisation in both Leinster and Meath seems to have been well under way.[32]

The actual process of colonisation has been studied in detail for Co. Meath only.[33] There Graham has indicated that settlement developed in two phases, which he has called "colonisation" and "spread". In the first phase military fortresses (mottes) were established in strategic dominating positions. The initial conquest was confined to immediate locations near mottes. The process of "spread" was more gradual and consisted of the establishment of manors as agricultural centres with markets, fairs, villages and towns developing subsequently.

The initial conquest was the work of a group of adventurers but once the ground became militarily stable the need arose for settlers and colonists who would work the new lands and make the adventurers' risk a profitable one. To do this not only villeins, but traders and artisans had also to be attracted. In the new territories, the privileges of the latter had to be at least as attractive as those which they left behind them. The adventurers offered burgess status to the potential town settlers.[34] In their foundation charters they granted a plot of land within the borough on which a house could be built; sometimes an acreage outside with access to the founders' woods; and a variety of privileges that included freedom of movement, the right of trial before equals, freedom from certain taxes and the right to participate in the governing of the town. The freedom and independent legal status thus offered also attracted large numbers of people who would otherwise have been tied to the land. In return the town founder received revenue in the form of an annual rent, market tolls and court fines; the town became a market place for the fruits of his soil and in time of trouble the loyalty of the townsmen could usually be relied on.

The origins of the settlers are uncertain. However, it does seem as if the south-west of England, in particular the lands around the Severn estuary, acted as a catchment area.[35]

The Site

The placename *droichead átha,* ford by the bridge, with its apparent conflict of meaning has caused much confusion. Between 1150 and 1210 the name was used in five different contexts. Firstly, it is evident from the annalistic entry of 1157 that *Drochat Átha* was a name applied to a large area rather than to a single feature such as a bridge or a ford.[36] Secondly it is used as a synonym for Mellifont Abbey.[37] Thirdly it is the name of one of the granges which formed part of the initial lands of the abbey.[38] Fourthly it is an area in which a church dedicated to St. Mary stands,[39] and lastly there is the *novus pons de Drogheda*, clearly the site of the present town.[40]

Fr. Colmcille has gone a long way towards explaining this diversity of meaning. By demonstrating that the grange of *Drochatatha* is to be identified with the grange of *vetera ponte*, otherwise Oldbridge, he has shown that the original ford lay considerably to the west of the modern town[41] and has given support to the identification made by Hogan in 1910.[42] He also points out that it was probably because Mellifont was the principal church in the Oldbridge locality that it came to be called *Mainistir*

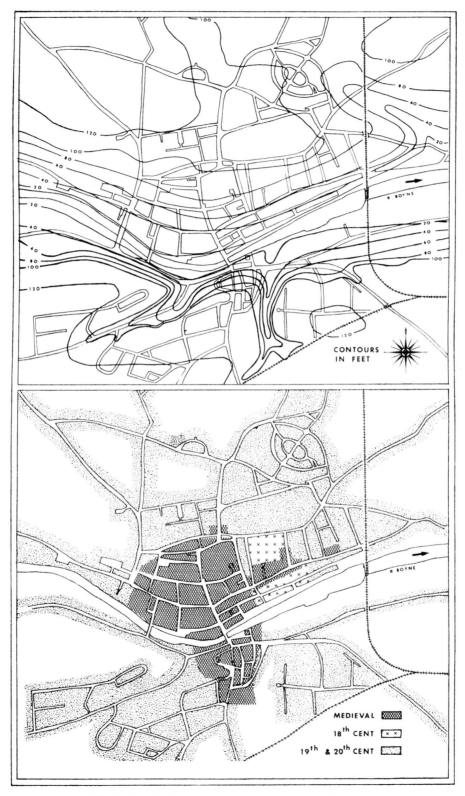

Fig 1. Drogheda: contour plan and growth phases.

Droichead Átha.[43] The church of St. Mary which Gwynn argued was later amalgamated with Mellifont[44] must also have been in the Oldbridge area. Perhaps it is significant that the abbots of Mellifont occasionally called themselves abbots of St. Mary's, Mellifont, or of Mellifont and Drogheda.[45] Most certainly the church of St. Mary of Drogheda cannot be identified with either of the two dedications to St. Mary within the medieval town both of which were in existence before the 'amalgamation' of St. Mary's with Mellifont.

The references to the new bridge provide the earliest positive evidence that the Anglo-Norman settlement was located away from the original *droichead átha* at Oldbridge. This mention of the *new* bridge is significant because it indicates that a new site was preferred to the already existing focal point that had been formed at the junction of the earlier routeways and the river crossing. Such a preference would indicate a deliberate choice in the selection of the new town site.

Neither the documentary nor the archaeological evidence indicates that there was any settlement at the town prior to the coming of the Normans. The references to Viking fleets in the ninth century state that they were on the Boyne,[46] but it seems extremely unlikely that any permanent settlement of the sort envisaged by D'Alton could have been established in this area with the royal centre of the kings of North Brega so close at Knowth.[47] The scatter of pre-Norman archaeological objects indicates nothing more than the presence of man in the neighbourhood over a long period of time. These objects include three Early Bronze Age flat axes, portion of a sword of Eogan's class 4 datable to c.700 b.c., and two penannular brooches probably of Early Christian date.[48] The coin hoard is regarded by Dolley as the earliest and probably the largest of the Irish coin hoards from the first half of the tenth century.[49] While the hoard was probably deliberately buried all of the other objects are more likely to have been lost casually. Besides it is not clear that the find place of any of them was within the walled town. The suggestion that the Millmount is a neolithic tumulus adapted as a motte may be dismissed for want of evidence, although it is probable that the greater part of the Boyne Valley mouth had been converted into cultivation land c.3000 b.c. by passage tomb builders.[50]

The Anglo-Norman town lay at a narrow bridging point on the tidal estuary of the river Boyne some five miles from the open sea. It occupies a fairly central location in the coastal plain formed by the Central Lowlands as it merges with the east coast. Along the south bank of the river there is a formidable scarp rising to a height of just over 100 feet (30.5m) with a gradient of I:7. The high ground of the scarp comes closest to the river at the bridging point, affording both a commanding view of the surrounding countryside as well as dominating the river crossing. The defensive advantages of the scarp were further increased by the presence of two ravines each carrying small streams, which formed a natural promontory overlooking the river. By contrast the land on the north side rises more gently with a gradient of I:23. This contrast in the land formations on each side of the river influenced the development of the town. The south side was ideal as a defensive site but the steep slope of the scarp constrained the spread of dwelling houses and shops. The north side on the other hand, was a level expanse suitable for the construction of houses and for the establishment of an extensive quayside.

The earliest archaeological feature is the Millmount motte, probably established by Hugh de Lacy before 1186.[51] De Lacy also seems to have been instrumental in setting up the two parish churches of the medieval town.[52] His connection with both churches is important because it shows him to be founder of the town on both sides of the Boyne and not just on the south side as has been previously thought.[53] Since the synod of Kells in 1152 the Boyne formed the boundary between the dioceses of Armagh and Meath. So two parishes had to be formed if the town was to be built on both sides of the river. Indeed it was largely because of this division that two separate towns emerged with independent corporations and privileges, and which only merged to form one town in 1412. St Peter's church was established on the north side before 1186 and was given by de Lacy to the Augustinian canons of Llanthony Prima in Monmouthshire,[54] while St. Mary's was given to its cell Llanthony Secunda in Gloucestershire.[55] These are both significant donations because Llanthony Prima was patronised, if not indeed founded, by the de Lacy family and in giving this addition to the Llanthony lands Hugh de Lacy was also ensuring that the Drogheda churches would be staffed with men from his own lands on the Welsh marches. The parish churches of the other de Lacy towns of Duleek and Trim were also maintained by Augustinian canons, and similarly with Navan which was seemingly established by one of de Lacy's tenants-in-chief Jocelin de Nangle.[56] The implication is that the Anglo-Norman adventurers found difficulty in obtaining regular clergy for their new settlements and had to bring in clergy from their homelands as part of the colonisation process.

The earliest surviving charter is one of 1194 to Drogheda in Meath.[57] In it Walter de Lacy confirms to all of his burgesses living on the south side of the bridge the law of Breuteil and further that each burgess may hold a burgage plot in which the front is fifty feet wide, as well as three acres in the fields outside the town; also that they may have free access along the Boyne as far as Trim with their boats. In return for these privileges the burgesses were to pay 12d. per annum to de Lacy. The law of Breteuil, a town in Normandy, consisting of a series of privileges originally conferred on that borough, was regarded as one of the best codes of burgess rights and was granted to new towns all over England, Wales and France. In Ireland it was given to Kells (Co. Meath), Duleek, Trim and Dungarvan among others.[58]

This charter emphasises the plantation nature of the new town of Drogheda. It is clear that colonists were being sought out, firstly from the offer of an internationally recognised set of burgess rights, secondly from the indication that there was a need to cultivate the soil as well as develop markets. The stipulation of burgage plot size indicates the deliberate thinking that went into the spatial organisation of the town. These factors taken together with the selection of a new site for the town, the setting up of two urban parishes and the importation of clergy to fill them show that Drogheda was being thought of as a town site in the 1180s. That is to say the town did not develop organically, rather that a decision was taken to found a town at this point in time. The recognition of Drogheda as a plantation town links it directly with the processes of town foundation and colonisation operating in Eastern Germany and in Gascony. It also places Hugh de Lacy into that international category of town developers found in twelfth and thirteenth century Europe which include the Lippe at Detmold and Lemgo in Westphalia and Edward I at New Winchelsea.

Internal Layout

The walled area of medieval Drogheda enclosed 113 acres (45 hectares) making it one of the largest walled towns in medieval Ireland. If one divides medieval towns into three broad area categories — large towns like Paris and London (over 160 acres), medium (80 - 160 acres), and small (under 80 acres), then Drogheda can be seen to fall into the middle grouping. Thus, while larger than Southampton it was comparable in size with Bristol, Oxford and Chichester and further afield with Arles, Limoges, Brno, Santiago de Compostella and Acre. In Ireland New Ross, Kilkenny and Dublin, including its suburbs, were of equivalent extent. The area enclosed by walls on the south side was 33 acres (13.2 hectares); and on the north side, 80 acres (32 hectares).

Much of the plot pattern within the walled town is a medieval survival and together with the street pattern is an example of how the town's past has survived *on* rather than above or below the ground. In this context it is important to realise that towns are ongoing monuments. Ongoing in that they are lived in and modified regularly; monuments in that in every age traces of their previous existence are visible within them. In this sense towns resemble buildings which are constructed and added to in different periods. Certain features have a greater and longer influence on the townscape than others. Streets, for instance, once established tend to remain sacrosanct as routeways for the duration of the

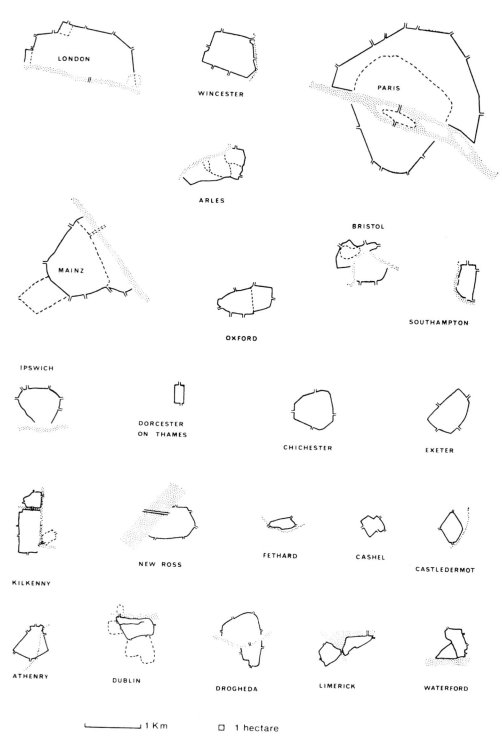

LONDON

WINCESTER

PARIS

ARLES

MAINZ

BRISTOL

OXFORD

SOUTHAMPTON

IPSWICH

DORCESTER
ON THAMES

CHICHESTER

EXETER

KILKENNY

NEW ROSS

FETHARD

CASHEL

CASTLEDERMOT

ATHENRY

DUBLIN

DROGHEDA

LIMERICK

WATERFORD

1 Km   □ 1 hectare

Fig.2: Drogheda and comparative medieval towns in north-western Europe.

town's existence. In a similar fashion property boundaries, once set up tend to be conservative features. It is to be expected that once a property has been formed the owner will take care to ensure that its boundaries are maintained. An example of such concern over a boundary line is the dispute between William Preston and William de Ellesworth about a strip of land two feet wide dividing their plots at Laurence Street (Great East Street) in 1311.[59] There they agreed to build a wall over the disputed boundary to a height of twelve feet.

The conservatism of property boundaries is particularly evident in some of the well documented English towns. At Oxford Salter was able to trace many of the individual house plots back to the thirteenth century.[60] Similar work has been done at Winchester and Southampton. Unfortunately, although almost one hundred tenement deeds survive for medieval Drogheda few of them can be positively identified with modern properties. One of the few is the messuage of Joneta Swayne, sister of the primate, which she held on the corner of Laurence Street and Freeschool Lane in 1436.[61] Others are indicated in fig. 3. Medieval tenement deeds defined the extent of the property by giving the names of the neighbouring owners rather than by dimensions. This means that even in streets for which one has a series of extant deeds, unless the neighbours can be identified it is not possible to identify the plots on the ground. This is the case with the many Preston properties in and around Shop (Bothe) Street.

The archaeological evidence for the continuity of property boundaries is very striking. At Dublin, Cork and Carrickfergus "modern" boundaries have been traced back one on top of the other down to the earliest levels.[62] Excavations at comparable towns in England have shown a similar pattern of continuity in the plots from the thirteenth until the nineteenth centuries.[63] Although both the archaeological and documentary sources indicate conservatism in the boundaries, it would be naive to assume that no changes took place. Not all proprietors were as conscientious about their holdings as William Preston and William de Ellesworth. The extent of the Irish lands of Llanthony Secunda, for instance, made in 1381 mentions that the monastery had many tenements in Drogheda on the south side of the Boyne, whose whereabouts were no longer known![64] In general however the *plot pattern* of individual holdings within the historic core, found on the first edition of the Ordnance Survey townplans (c. 1840) is most likely a survival of the medieval pattern.

Drogheda in Meath

Much of the original street pattern has been interfered with but comparison with Newcomen's and Ravell's map show the pattern before the construction of Mary Street. The plan was composed of two main north-south streets — Pitcher Hill and Curry's Hill — and one east-west route, James's Street and John Street. Cornmarket Hill may also have been a medieval street but there is no positive evidence remaining. Newcomen indicates that a route continued westwards along the line of the present day Barrack Street and along the back of the John Street plots to the Butter Gate.

Although it is likely that much of the south side had been settled before Walter de Lacy made his grant of 1194, the earliest reference to a street does not occur until c. 1260 when, by inference, John Street is mentioned.[65] The street is specifically named in 1317[66] and Robert Preston held three properties there in the mid-fourteenth century.[67] The burgage plot pattern is still largely intact on the north side of the street, but the form of all of the properties on the south side was destroyed during the construction of the new road in 1976. The O.S. maps of the last century show that the holdings on both sides of the street were of the long burgage plot variety, i.e. one in which the ratio between plot length and breadth is more than 5:1. This sort of plot, which was very common in medieval Irish towns, is also present in Duleek Street. The Hospital of St. John the Baptist maintained by the Fratres Cruciferi, lay at the west end of the street probably on the south side.[68] D'Alton says that it was established by Walter de Lacy but he quotes no source.[69] At the time he wrote some walls were still standing but nothing now remains.[70] It seems to have stood within its own precinct walls and is described in 1475-6 as being outside the walls of the town.[71] Maher suggested that a building shown on one of Place's drawings may have been part of this hospital.[72]

James's Street is not referred to as far as I am aware until 1467 when several burgage plots valued at 10s. per annum belonging to the Carmelite friary of St. Mary the Virgin are mentioned.[73] The Tholsel stood at the west end of this street on the corner with Pitcher Hill.[74] It later became known as the "Castle of Comfort" or "Castle of Drogheda."[75] It is shown as a tower house on Newcomen's map of 1657. The Hospital of St. James stood within its own precinct wall outside the town on the north side of the street.[76] D'Alton places its foundation at the close of the thirteenth century,[77] but gives no source for this assertion. In effect nothing at all is known of its origin, function or history during this period.

In James's Street there is a street block segmented by plot divisions suggesting that these holdings had a front to the street and another to the quays. Much of this block is at present scheduled for destruction in order to link the new road with the Dublin road. Shops near the quays are mentioned in 1354 and 1363.[78] St. Mary's Hill is referred to in a deed of 1363.[79] Moira Corcoran has suggested that it may be identified with Pitcher Hill[80] but St. Mary's Lane (on Ravell's map, since destroyed) is to be preferred since it is closer to the church. The same deed refers to the "street leading from the town leading towards the Carmelite Friars" which is most likely to be identified with Curry's Hill (Ravell's Scarlet Lane).[81] It is not possible to identify the exact whereabouts of the plots belonging to Christ Church (Dublin), Tristernagh or the monastery of Holcultram (Cumbria) except to say that they were on this side of the town.[82]

The broad wedge-shaped space where James's Street, Pitcher Hill and John Street converge in front of the Tholsel, known as the Bullring, immediately suggests itself as the market place of the town. The date of the 'Cornmarket' half way up Cornmarket Hill is unknown.

Within the grounds of St. Mary's stood a complex of ecclesiastical structures: the parish church itself, the church of St. Nicholas and the Carmelite friary of St. Mary. The parish church as already mentioned was established by Hugh de Lacy and given to Llanthony Secunda. It is called *ecclesiam de Novo Ponte* c.1202 and *ecclesiam Sancte Marie de Ponte* c 1211.[83] It had at least three chapels attached to it, dedicated to the Blessed Virgin, St. Catherine and St. Patrick.[84] The church is named along with St. Patrick's and Christ Church (Dublin) as one of the three churches in Ireland in which the plenary indulgence of Sextus IV could be obtained in 1477.[85] The church of St. Nicholas may have been established as early as St. Mary's on which it seems to have been dependent.[86] The earliest specific mention occurs c. 1211.[87] It had an upper chamber and a cellar which were used for storage purposes by the Llanthony canons.[88] In 1393 three shops are referred to as "near St. Nicholas's church"; these may have been on church lands.[89] D'Alton contended that the Carmelite friary was established by the townsmen but there is no evidence to support this.[90] Indeed of its form and precise location within the church grounds nothing is known. The extent of the friary made in 1540 says that all of its buildings were thrown down then which may indicate that they were not as substantial as those of the parish church.[91]

Place's drawing shows the church buildings that survived the Cromwellian assault of 1649. These include portion of a substantial tower located at least half way down the church, implying the presence of a long chancel. The tower, present on Ricciardelli's picture, had fallen by 1791 when Grose's print was prepared.[92] The fragmentary structure standing to the south of the present church was regarded by Davies as of recent date, and indeed looks very like the roofed building in Grose's print.[93] There are a number of carved mouldings, mullions and window jambs built into a cross wall in the graveyard, all of which are of fourteenth-fifteenth century date.[94] The tower was also most likely of this date and suggests that the church was substantially rebuilt at that time.

Drogheda is exceptional among the major Irish medieval towns in that its motte was never replaced by a stone castle. At present the motte has an average external diameter of 60m at the base and 28m

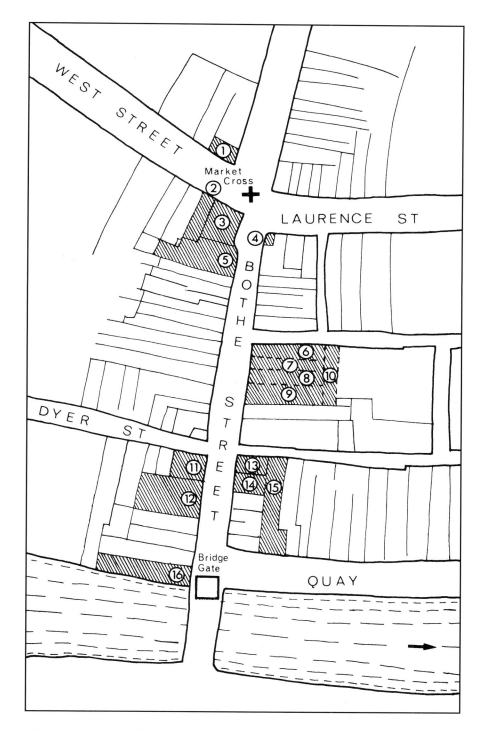

Fig. 3 The location of some of the identifiable medieval properties in Drogheda: (1) Llanthony Canons of St. Peter c. 1250; Laundy's Castle c.1600. (2) Roger de Preston 1342. (3) Tholsel. (4) Bathe House 1570. (5) Llanthony Canons of St. Mary's 1381. (6), (7) William de Preston 1319. (8) John le Boweneys 1319. (9) John Cosyn 1319. (10) Richard Burgeys, Adam Heyroun 1319; Henry Lumbyn 1321. (11) Robert de Preston 1355. (12) Llanthony Canons of St. Peter's 1355. (13) Alexander Preston 1363. (14) Henry le Boweneys 1363. (15) Martin Johan 1363. (16) Chapel of St. Saviour's.

at the top. There were two baileys. The upper bailey was somewhat elliptical in shape and had maximum dimensions of 75m long by 50m broad. It was connected with the motte by a timber bridge.[95] The lower bailey was roughly rectangular in shape with maximum dimensions of 60m long by 30m broad. Within both baileys at present are buildings associated with the military barracks constructed in the mid-eighteenth century. Orpen suggested that the hall chapel and prison would have been situated in the baileys.[96] The castle was taken over by the Crown early in the thirteenth century because it was regarded as too important to remain in private hands. In 1381 John Asshewell, controller of customs in the port of Drogheda was given a grant of the vacant plot known as the "Castlemote of Drogheda" together with custody of an empty stone tower and was given licence to build a windmill thereon and also a dove-cote.[97]

The defences of the upper bailey were linked directly with those of the town. The modern bailey wall runs right up the side of the motte but it is unlikely that this is an original feature. It is evident from Isaac Butler's description and some eighteenth century prints that the base of the motte, on the east (town) side was subsequently surrounded by a wall with five stone towers.[98]

The town wall on the south side had four gates and six or seven mural towers. The uncertainty in the number of mural towers is due to the unclear nature of their depiction on Newcomen's map. Of the four gates, only a portion of one – the Butter Gate – remains. This consists now of a single arch with maximum surviving dimension of 8m in breadth and 10.2m in height. An octagonal tower rose from the gateway which was only removed in this century.[99] The name "Butter Gate" would seem to be a corruption of Bebeck's Gate alias Butress Gate.[100] To the north of the Butter Gate stood St. John's Gate which, on the basis of Place and Ricciardelli would seem to have been a large rectangular gatehouse. The Duleek Gate on the south side of the town is mentioned during the mid-fourteenth century.[101] St. James's Gate on the east side is first referred to, as far as I am aware, in 1540.[102] It would appear to have stood just to the east of the junction between James's Street and Curry's Hill. Newcomen's map shows river towers at the east and west of the junction between the wall and the river. Traces of these were still present when the O.S. cartographers prepared their plans in the last century. Immediately to the south of the Millmount, Newcomen shows a tower which could have functioned as a gate. Goche's map places towers at the south east and south west angles, and Newcomen shows three towers on the east wall between St. Mary's Church and St. James's Gate. It is not possible to plot these features except in a very rough manner.

Drogheda in Louth

The medieval street pattern has survived almost completely intact into modern times. The plan is of chequer form with four streets running parallel to the river, intersected by one main north-south route and a series of cross streets. None of the chequers thus formed is laid out with any sort of mathematical precision such as chequers of New Winchelsea or the Gascon 'bastide' towns.

The earliest reference to a street on the north side is to Bothe (Shop) Street mentioned in 1214.[103] The name is derived from the booths or shops which would have been found in this street, and may be compared with the Bothe Street in Dublin. Towards the end of the thirteenth century the Llanthony canons were receiving dues from a *placea* (plot) on the west side of the street, perhaps to be identified with the plot held by them in 1355.[104] The names of tenants for six plots on the east of the street and five on the west are known during the fourteenth century and some of these can be pinpointed exactly.[105] On the south side of the junction between Batchelor's Lane and Shop Street (where the open area in front of the Augustinian friary lies) stood two Preston properties to the south of which lay a tenement of le Boweneys and next to that one belonging to the Cosyns. Unfortunately all trace of these was removed during the construction of the present friary. On the south side of the junction with

Gabriele Ricciardelli, fl. 1743 - 1782
View of Drogheda From Ball's Grove. See Footnote 1.
Property of the Corporation of Drogheda.

We are looking towards the sea. On the right is the tower of the Carmelite Friary, where St. Mary's Church (C. of I.) now stands. Below this is the 3-arched bridge, erected in 1722. Across the river, on the slope of the hill, is St. Laurence's Gate. On the skyline are St. Peter's Church (C. of I.) erected in 1752 and the Magdalene Tower, with Sunday's Gate in between them. A number of other gates can be seen along the town wall.

This picture of Drogheda with its fortifications by Van der Hag[e]
fireplace in the Great Hall. The view approximates closely t[o]

...as commissioned for Beaulieu, to be set in a recess over the stone
...ardelli but shows the older 2-arched bridge. See footnote 16.

Gabriele Ricciardelli, fl. 1743-1782.
View of Drogheda. See Footnote 1.
Oil on Canvas, 71 x 151 cms
Property of the Corporation of Drogheda.

Ricciardelli, born in Naples, came to Dublin for a brief period in 1753, before spending some years in England. He painted portraits and landscapes. It is for the latter that he is known to-day, his Irish scenes being distinguished by his excellently accurate portrayal of architectural features. This view of Drogheda is taken from the Millmount, looking westwards up river, with the town of Drogheda on the right. The large building on the left is the barracks and beyond that is Ball's Grove.

Bessexwell Lane lay another Preston property, next to which on the south was another belonging to le Boweneys. The Prestons also held a house across from this, on the south side of the junction with Dyer Street, with the Llanthony canons directly to the south of them. These latter plots still survive.

On the south west end of the street beside the bridge lay St. Saviour's chapel (alias the chapel of the Holy Redeemer). It would seem to have been maintained by the Llanthony canons of St. Peter's and functioned as a chantry or perhaps a sort of chapel of ease.[106] The cellars beneath the chapel, first mentioned in 1294, were still being used in 1745.[107] Newcomen's map shows it simply as a church with a tower. It was set back some 12-14 feet from Shop Street.[108] The chapel is first mentioned in 1218.[109] The quay of the Llanthony canons lay directly to the south of the chapel.[110]

The Tholsel stood at the north west end of the street and the tenement of the parish church of St. Mary, mentioned in the extent of 1381, probably lay to the south of it since the Prestons held the property on the west.[111] There were also cellars beneath the Tholsel which were also held by the Llanthony canons of St. Mary's.[112] The Tholsel was occasionally referred to as the Guildhall.[113] It is shown on Newcomen's plan as a tower house.

The change in name from East Street to St. Laurence Street seems to have occurred about 1350, but the existence of the street may be inferred from a charter of c. 1206 mentioning the East Gate of the town.[114] The street is not specifically named until the middle of the thirteenth century when both stone and timber houses are mentioned there.[115] A plot belonging to the Hospital of St. John the Baptist Dublin is referred to in 1298.[116] The names of nine tenants on the north side of the street and of eleven on the south side survive from the fourteenth century.[117] Only one of these can be tentatively identified – the plot of John FitzRobert which would appear to have been the final plot on the south side of the street and separated from the town wall by the lane leading to St. Elena's well.[118] The house of John Jordan is mentioned in 1396 and was perhaps connected with the clothier of the same name two generations before.[119] Two plots are referred to in the fifteenth century, of which that belonging to Joneta Swayne on the west side of Freeschool (Frumboldes) Lane may still be identified.[120] Frobolles Inn also stood in this street.[121] Indeed in view of the similarity of the name it may have been located on the east end of Frumboldes Lane. There is also the possibility that the "particularly skilled goldsmith" who repaired the cross of Michael Tregury, archbishop of Dublin, had his workshop in this area.[122]

It may be inferred from the charter of the house of St. Mary d'Urso *extra portam occidentalem de Droheda* that West Street was in existence before c. 1214.[123] References to properties in the street are few. The house at Schwer's corner, later known as Laundy's Castle, was granted to the Llanthony canons of St. Peter c. 1250.[124] There are only two fourteenth century tenement deeds, from which the two tenants immediately to the west of the Tholsel in 1342 can be identified as Preston and Bretnagh.[125] William Warant held a hall here in 1407,[126] and the "house of the scholars of Drogheda" lay towards the west end of the street in 1452.[127] The fountain known as St. Patrick's well was also located in this vicinity.[128] The Tholsel Inn mentioned in 1521 was presumably situated near the Tholsel on the east end of the street.[129] All of the surviving burgage plots on this street, as in Laurence Street, are of the long variety except where they make the junction with Shop Street and Peter Street.

Peter Street, known as Great North Street, is first mentioned in 1331.[130] The Prestons held four properties here during the mid fourteenth century and the house of St. Mary d'Urso had at least one.[131] Of the other streets for which there is documentary evidence the earliest is the road near the *porta septentrionalis* mentioned in the mid-thirteenth century and which can be identified with Magdalene Street.[132] The westward extension of this street, now known as the Rope Walk, is mentioned in a deed of 1341.[133] Irish Street, the *vicus hibernicorum*, is referred to in three fourteenth century deeds, from which it is evident that it ran in an east-west direction and so should be identified with Green Lane and not Bolton Street as Moira Corcoran has suggested.[134] It is noteworthy that of the thirteen tenants named in these deeds not one of them has a diagnostically Irish name and the Prestons who held some of these tenements are a demonstrably English family.

The Prestons held nine properties in Bachelors Lane and in the deeds relating to them the names of fifteen tenants on the north side of the lane and seven on the south side are preserved.[135] Of these, the position of the plot which Henry Lumbyn held in 1321 can alone be tentatively identified. It would appear to have stood on the south side of the lane immediately beside the Preston property on the corner with Shop Street (supra). The Augustinian Friary now covers the site. The Cistercian house of St. Mary, Dublin held at least two properties in Bessexwell Lane while the Prestons had four.[136] Some of the plots on the south side of this lane spanned the width of the street block and had one front on the lane and another on the quays. One of these properties may be still plotted: that of Martin Johan in 1363 which lay on the south side of the lane beside the Preston plot on the Shop Street corner.[137]

Dyer Street is first mentioned in 1329 and in a subsequent deed of 1355 it is called the *vicus tinctorum* indicating that this area, close to the fresh water of the Boyne, was one in which clothiers worked.[138] There are three fourteenth century property deeds relating to Fair Street but the whereabouts of the plots can no longer be determined.[139] The Hospital of St. John the Baptist also held a plot in this street.[140] Houses in Stockwell's Lane, William Street, Freeschool Lane and on the quays are also recorded.[141]

The lane which led from Laurence Street to St. Elena's well mentioned in 1351 is probably to be identified with the lane just inside the town wall, now a cul-de-sac.[142] Perhaps it is the same as the lane referred to in two earlier documents which also ran southwards from Laurence Street.[143] The St. Bride Street mentioned in the early sixteenth century was probably a subdivision of Laurence Street.[144] A "blind lane" near Shop Street is mentioned in a deed of 1318,[145] but its location like that of the Furnace Lane referred to c. 1230 and the early sixteenth century Fyshehambels, can no longer be determined.[146]

The principal market place was located in front of the Tholsel at the junction of Shop Street, Peter Street, West Street and Laurence Street, known as the "cross of the town". A market cross was set up here in 1501 and is shown on Goche's map.[147] It functioned not just as a centre for transacting business, but was also the place where proclamations were read.[148] The pillory was probably sited here.[149] It seems likely that the wide space in front of St. Peter's church functioned as a subsidiary market place. The date of the potato market and the hay and milk market is uncertain.

Apart from St. Saviour's chapel there were six churches on the north side and of these the parish church of St. Peter and the Franciscan Friary stood within the wall. The Dominican friary and the hospital of St. Mary d'Urso stood within their own precincts, which were incorporated into the town defences, and the hospital of St. Laurence stood outside the wall on the east. The exact whereabouts of the Augustinian friary remains uncertain. D'Alton confused it with the hospital of St. Mary d'Urso but it is clear from the suppression documents that it was distinct.[150]

The Llanthony canons, brought in to administer St. Peter's, had their parish rights confirmed by successive archbishops of Armagh throughout the period.[151] Gravedigging in the churchyard has recovered wall foundations which suggest that the medieval church stood slightly to the east of the present building which dates from 1749-52.[152] From Butler's account the cruciform church would appear to have had a long nave of ten bays, with north and south aisles, a tower at the crossing and a chancel flanked by two large side chapels, opening presumably off the transepts.[153] The church had at least seven chapels dedicated to St. Mary, St. John, St. Anne, St. Martin, St. Catherine, St. George and St. Patrick, but only the first four of these can definitely be assigned to the medieval period.[154] The location of the chapel of St. Anne is described exactly as being on the north side of the chancel.[155] No architectural information can be gathered from the drawings of Goche, Place or Newcomen. The fragmentary Register of the Mayors of Drogheda indicates that there was sizable structural alteration in the early sixteenth century. In 1515 the window of St. Mary's chapel was erected and in 1525 the south aisle was built.[156] The tower described by a contemporary inhabitant of Drogheda as "one of the highest steeples in the world" fell in 1548.[157] The octagonal font which has been dated to this time by Roe is further evidence for substantial patronage of the church immediately before the Reformation.[158] Of the handful of cut stones which survive from the medieval church a portion of a double cusped light could also date to this time.[159] Inside the church, in the vestry wall, is a bracket, possibly of thirteenth century date.[160]

A school of Drogheda mentioned in conjunction with St. Peter's in 1233 was perhaps located near the churchyard.[161] Throughout the period under consideration this church functioned as a pro-cathedral and was used by the Armagh primates for holding synods; many of the primates were also buried there.[162] The "old palace" described in 1417 as within the graveyard of St. Peter's was presumably the place of residence of the archbishops of Armagh while at Drogheda.[163] About 1470 permission was granted to construct buildings along the glebe wall, which may perhaps be identified with the small plots on the Peter Street side of the churchyard.[164] A house of the sick beside St. Peter's is mentioned in 1388, and it would seem as if provision was made at the beginning of the thirteenth century to have a residence within the church grounds for the Llanthony monks.[165] To the north of the church, between the graveyard wall and Magdalene Street, the house of St. John the Baptist Dublin held a plot of land in the mid-thirteenth century.[166] The same monastery also held land to the west of the church, and properties were held near the churchyard by the hospital of St. Mary d'Urso and the Abbey of Furness.[167]

No trace of the Franciscan friary survives. Its location however, can be determined on the basis of references in the *Gormanston Register* and in the seventeenth century Mooney manuscripts. The precincts extended from the river on the south to Bachelors Lane on the north, and from the town wall on the east to the present Custom House on the west.[168] The convent hospital stood beside the river bank and the church itself was probably nearer to Bachelors Lane.[169] According to Fr. Mooney the east window of the church pierced the town wall and looked out onto the friary orchard.[170] It had a high tower of cut stone, similar to others of the order in Ireland and probably of fifteenth century date.[171] The site itself was low lying and susceptible to flooding, and the friary seems to have been badly damaged in the great flood of 1330.[172] Its buildings were large and sumptuous enough to entertain royalty, and it was here that Richard II stayed for eighteen days in 1394.[173] A *domo consilii regis* is mentioned in 1444 and was presumably a large room in which the king's council could meet.[174] Apart from the tower, additional evidence for fifteenth century rebuilding is evident from the repair of some of the church windows in 1437.[175] The friary had a noted school of theology in the second quarter of the fifteenth century, and it has been suggested that its fame was one of the reasons for the choice of Drogheda as the centre for an Irish university in 1465.[176] It cannot be determined however if this school was housed in a separate building. No tombslabs survive, nor is the site of the cemetery known. In the early seventeenth century however there appears to have been at least one carved table tomb in the choir.[177] According to Ware the monastery was founded c. 1240, but the earliest extant reference to the Franciscans at Drogheda is one of 1245.[178]

The Magdalen tower is the only surviving remnant of the Dominican friary established c. 1224 by Luke Netterville, archbishop of Armagh.[179] The precinct seems to have been large and a glance at Newcomen's map indicates an enclosed area between Upper Magdalene Street and Patrick Street, adjoining the town wall. The buildings appear to have been extensive, and the drawing of "St. Sunday's Friary" reproduced by D'Alton is undoubtedly part of the Dominican foundation.[180] The drawing shows an arcaded nave with aisles. The tower stood presumably between the nave and chancel which was dedicated to the Blessed Virgin Mary.[181] It has a high pointed arch on each side with groined vaulting. The gable coping of the chancel survives and above it are the double-cusped pointed lights of the ringing stage. The windows of the belfry stage are twin double-cusped transomed lights. Above the top cornice are stepped battlements. Access to the upper stages was via a stair in a projecting square turret on the north-west side. Within the friary precinct was a hospital dedicated to St. Mary Magdalen and it is likely that the friary was built on the site of the chapel of St. Mary Magdalen mentioned c. 1206.[182] The burials excavated by Etienne Rynne in this vicinity were perhaps part of the friary cemetery.[183] A number of line impressed floor tiles of fifteenth century date have been found, some of which have affinites with examples in the Chester area.[184] None of these tiles appear to have been found *in situ* however. Like the tiles, the Magdalen tower is of fifteenth century date, perhaps constructed shortly after 1467-8 when the friary received an annual grant from the Irish parliament to carry out repairs.[185]

The hospital of St. Mary d'Urso lay at the western end of the town, and when founded actually lay without the West Gate. Portions of the chancel, nave and tower of the church survive. D'Alton and Kelly regarded the site as that of an early Patrician church.[186] This is based on its confusion with Trevet, Co. Meath, whereas there is in fact no reliable evidence to indicate that there was a church on this site prior to the thirteenth century. The same writers regarded the church as belonging later to the Franciscans or Augustinians, but again it is clear from the extents made at the time of the Dissolution that the hospital was not associated with either order.[187] The hospital was established c. 1206-1214 by Ursus de Swemele, burgess of Drogheda, and a group of charters survives relating to its foundation.[188] From these it can be seen that before founding the hospital Ursus negotiated with both the corporation of the town and the Llanthony canons who administered St. Peter's parish. Of its subsequent history little is known, but it is clear from the surviving buildings that in the fifteenth century it was sufficiently wealthy to build a tower onto the church. The tower has two tall pointed arches with two orders and plain bevels springing from piers four feet wide. Above the main vault the tower is slightly set back on the east and west sides and the gable-coping of chancel and nave can be seen. The belfry stage was lit by four two-light transomed and mullioned windows with cusped ogee heads. The stair was placed in a projecting rectangular turret on the south-east side. The south wall of the nave survives for a length of about fifteen feet (5m), but most of the nave and chancel have been destroyed by a lane which runs through the church. A blocked-up window at the west end of the nave suggests the presence of an aisle on the north side, and a nave length of approximately ninety feet (27.5m) can be estimated. Most of the south wall of the chancel survives although the north wall is present only in fragments. There was a large pointed window in the east gable of which the internal ashlar jambs survive. A round headed doorway in the south wall gave access to the tower stair. Davies has already given the internal dimensions of the chancel as 76ft. 4ins. (23.3m) by 24ft. 9ins. (7.5m).[189]

The location of the Augustinian friary is uncertain. A mention in an eighteenth century lease suggests that it was in the vicinity of the hospital of St. Mary d'Urso, perhaps on the east side of Dominick Street.[190] At the Supression the friars owned no land apart from that on which the monastery stood.[191]

D'Alton has already suggested that the Cord church should be identified with the church of the hospital of St. Laurence, and I agree with him on this.[192] The apparent distance of the site from the walled town can be accounted for by the fact that the eastern suburbs extended eastwards at least as far as Oulster Lane which can be identified with the fourteenth century Lythirwethir Lane.[193] It appears unlikely that another church would have existed between Oulster Lane and the Cord cemetery. The hospital seems to have been established c.1206 when it was moved to a location outside the East Gate from the chapel of St. Mary Magdalen.[194] It may have been established, as D'Alton believed, by the townsmen but little is known of its organisation or layout, although the names of

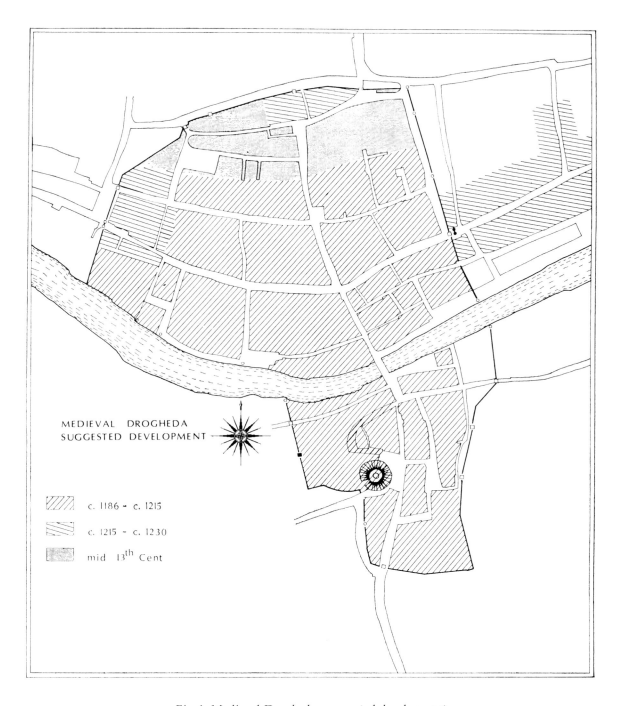

MEDIEVAL DROGHEDA
SUGGESTED DEVELOPMENT

c. 1186 – c. 1215

c. 1215 – c. 1230

mid 13th Cent

Fig 4. Medieval Drogheda: suggested development

some of the priors survive. By the mid-fifteenth century much of the building fabric seems to have been in disrepair.[195] The extant remains consist of the east gable wall of the church together with a medieval gargoyle with a distorted face spout and arms on the lower side.[196]

Although the lines of the town walls can be determined with reasonable exactness, the number of gates and towers, together with the position of some, remains uncertain. The basic sources are the series of early maps and the topographical drawings which, as already stated, vary in accuracy and detail. Goche's sketch for instance shows four gates and seven towers; Newcomen's has five gates, ten towers and a river wall while Ravell like Goche has four gates and seven towers, but in different positions. The only surviving remains are a portion of the wall on the west side, the barbican of St. Laurence's Gate and portion of the wall near it. While the position of the gates is self-evident in most cases, the precise location of the towers can be determined solely by excavation, and on the accompanying map only their approximate position is shown.

The west wall appears to have lacked mural towers, but it had two if not three gates. The West Gate appears from both Place and Ricciardelli to have had a twin bastioned barbican very similar to St. Laurence's with the gate itself lying inside. Ricciardelli's portrayal of the Fair Gate suggests that it was a rectangular structure similar to the Tholsel Gate at Carlingford or the North Gate at Athenry. Newcomen indicates that there was a gate at the west end of the Rope Walk, but it may have been nothing more than a tower. The greater part of the north wall was composed of curtain wall alone, but there were at least two towers, and St. Sunday's Gate which derived its name from St. Sunday's Friary, an alternative name for the Dominican house. This gate, the subject of two drawings by Place, was a rectangular structure similar to those already mentioned at Carlingford and Athenry and had a barbican linked to the tower by two side walls with a single arched bridge spanning the town ditch.[197] The barbican was not as elaborate as those of the West Gate or St. Laurence's Gate but it would have served to confine attackers into a limited space where they would have been easy prey for defenders in the gatehouse. No trace of the structure now survives although portion was still forming the wall of a forge when D'Alton wrote.[198] In thirteenth and fourteenth century documents the gate is referred to as the "North Gate" or the "Cow Gate".[199] In plan and function this gate resembled the Walmgate Bar at York.[200]

The names of the towers along the east wall survive on Ravell's map: Tooting (or Shooting) Tower stood at the junction of the north and east walls; Taylors Hall, portion of which was still standing at the rear of No. 13 King Street in 1941,[201] and Pigeon Tower were to the north of St. Laurence's Gate. An early view suggests that they were all circular or semi-circular bastions.[202]

St. Laurence's Gate derived its name from the fact that it stood across the road leading to the hospital of St. Laurence, but prior to the mid-fourteenth century it was known simply as the East Gate.[203] Nothing survives of the gatehouse itself but the barbican is the most magnificent remnant of medieval town defences to survive in Ireland. It consists of two almost circular drum towers flanking a low entrance arch. Though the towers are similar in appearance they are not identical and the southern tower projects more to the east than the northern one. There was an entrance up a flight of steps in each tower and access to the upper storeys was attainable from either. There were four floors in each tower with a crenellated parapet at the top. The two towers were joined at parapet level by a bridge which enabled movement between them. The exterior face presents a defensible front to the main approach from the east and the sea. The interior face is little less defensible in character than the east front, and could have held off attack from inside the town as equally as from without. The entrance had a portcullis and wooden gates. There is no trace of a chamber above the gate to house the winding gear for raising the portcullis and the manner of lifting it remains unclear. The barbican dates to the

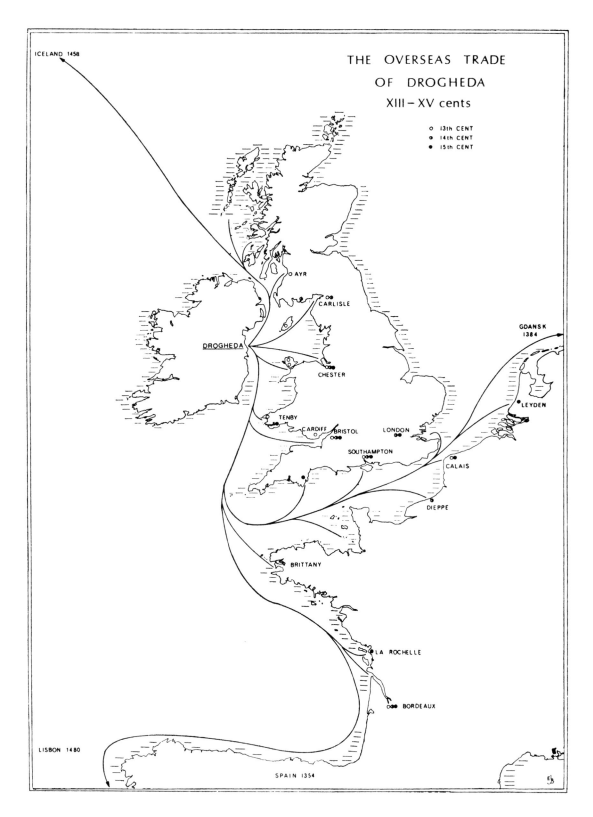

Fig. 5 The overseas trade of Drogheda.

mid-thirteenth century and compares well with some of the more impressive English gateways such as the West Gate at Cantebury and is larger, for instance, than the Landgate at Rye.[204]

South of St. Laurence's Gate there was a Blind Gate at the end of Bachelors Lane which probably functioned as a postern for the Franciscans. South of this and almost on the quay was St. Catherine's Gate. The wall alongside the quay seems to have been purely a curtain wall on the east side of the bridge. The bridge itself however was protected by a gate. Newcomen shows five towers on the quay wall west of the bridge.

Drogheda possesses one of the most extensive series of murage grants for any Irish town with at least thirteen grants spanning the 190 years between 1234 and 1424. The murage grant was the principal source of revenue for any town wishing to build a wall. Basically it consisted of a licence to levy a toll (called murage) upon goods coming into the town and the monies thus gathered were used to construct the wall. Murage was granted after application by the townsmen to the king. The first grants in England were issued during the 1220s and were given on limited conditions for periods of about three years. By the end of the thirteenth century the period had lengthened to ten years and by the middle of the fourteenth century twenty was common. In the initial grants the list of taxable articles was short and the rate was low but gradually the list lengthened and the rate increased.[205] These developments can also be seen in the Drogheda examples. The known grants are as follows: 1234-37, 1243-45, 1278-81, 1296-1303, 1307-12, 1317-22, 1333-39, 1339-49, 1356-62, 1362-82, 1373-82, 1385-97, 1402-24.[206] Apart from these, direct grants of money were made in 1322 and 1442.[207] Unfortunately the murage grants are not sufficient in themselves to give an idea of the building campaigns, or of how quickly the wall went up. Neither are the surviving portions of the defences extensive enough to fill out such a picture as is the case at Kilkenny where the period of building has been suggested as c. 1250-1352.[208] It may well be that the initial defences of the town were of earth and timber; certainly the East Gate referred to c. 1206 cannot be the present stone gate which was not started until at least half a century later.[209] The barbican of St. Laurence's Gate indicates that large scale building was in progress during the mid to late thirteenth century, while the series of fourteenth and early fifteenth century murage grants show that the wall was being kept in repair.

There were suburbs outside the walls on the north and east sides, and possibly on the west also. The earliest and largest of these was the eastern suburb situated outside St. Laurence's Gate and stretching along the present Cord Road. Its original extent is uncertain but in the fourteenth century it continued eastwards at least as far as the present Oulster Lane (see p. 18). Burgages outside the East Gate are first referred to in a deed of c. 1230.[210] the northern suburb is known from a single mid-fourteenth century reference in which a messuage, seven shops and a garden are described as lying outside the Cow Gate.[211] The possibility of a western suburb is suggested by the fact that the hospital of St. Mary d'Urso when established lay outside the wall but was subsequently incorporated within it together with the northern portion of Narrow West Street, where there is only house plot evidence. This suggests that hospital and houses originally lay outside an early wall and thus formed a suburb.

Plan Development

From the detailed examination of the medieval topography a generalised picture of Drogheda's early development may be formed. Firstly the site itself appears to have been new. The lack of any pre-thirteenth century finds from the town together with the name *novus pons* and the almost certain identification of the twelfth century fording place at *Droichead Átha* as Oldbridge all indicate an absence of settlement prior to the founding of the town by Hugh de Lacy. The initial importance of the site was strategic - control of the bridging point; but the site had commercial advantages also. Apart from being a crossing point and thus at the meeting of routes, there was easy access from the

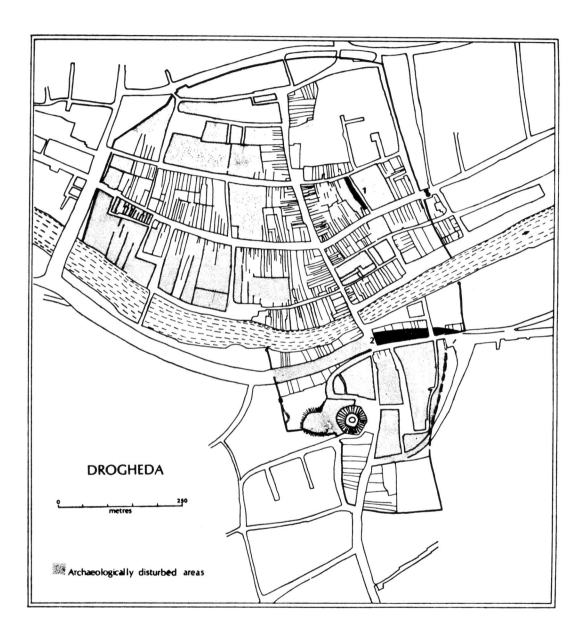

Fig.6 The archaeological potential of medieval Drogheda. The areas in which disturbance has occurred during the recent past are shaded. In some cases the disturbances is confined to the upper layers only and stratified deposits are probably present beneath. The churchyards of St. Mary's and St. Peter's are not shaded but disturbance in the form of burials has occurred there. The sites in black are under immediate threat. No.1 is a private development on the site of a known plot of 1436. No. 2 shows the line of the proposed road widening.

DROGHEDA

0   250
metres

Archaeologically disturbed areas

sea, and the river into the hinterland was navigable for almost twenty miles. The town was divided into two parts, north (Louth, Uriel) and south (Meath) of the river, probably from its foundation. The creation of two parishes and Walter de Lacy's charter to his burgesses of Drogheda *in Meath* suggest that this partition was early. In this respect Drogheda had some of the characteristics of a twin town - established on a boundary, rivalry between the corporations and substantial rents accruing to the lord, at first the de Lacys and subsequently the Crown.[212] Both sides of the river were clearly being colonised by 1194, and the early references to Shop Street, West Street and Laurence Street show that the basic axis of the town on the north side - which is still the town's principal business area - was established before 1215. The mention of the East Gate c. 1206 suggests that the town was already fortified, probably with earthen ramparts, and that it had reached eastwards as far as the present St. Laurence's Gate by this time. Further evidence for this is seen c. 1230 when the existence of a suburb outside of the East Gate is evident. That settlement had spread westwards as far as the entrance to Narrow West Street by 1214 is clear from the establishment of the hospital of St. Mary d'Urso "outside the West Gate" around this time. The northern limit of the town at this stage remains uncertain, but it must have included St. Peter's parish church established before 1186 and most likely did not extend as far as the leper hospital of St. Mary Magdalen (on the site of the later Dominican house) mentioned c. 1206. It was presumably when settlement began to encroach on this hospital that its site was moved and the priory of St. Laurence established. The expansion of the town after c. 1215, in so far as it can be traced, consisted of little more than incorporation of the religious precincts on the north and west sides within the wall i.e. the hospital of St. Mary d'Urso and the Dominican Friary. The development of the town on the south side of the Boyne was largely influenced by its geographical setting, and settlement could really only take place along the flat ground fronting the river side at the base of the scarp.

The remarkable point about Drogheda is that so much of it was established within the generation from c. 1186 - c.1215. when this is taken together with the evidence from Kilkenny where the greater part of the medieval town was established by c. 1220[213] it becomes clear that the Anglo-Norman colonisation of Ireland between 1170 and 1220 must have occurred on a massive scale, particularly in the urban areas. Furthermore this emphasises the plantation nature of Anglo-Norman town foundation whereby sites were populated with a new stock of people over a short space of time. The selection of a new site in preference to the old one, the establishment of new parishes, the early grant of privileges and the rapid development of the site all indicate that Drogheda was a planted town. It is not however a Bastide town. It is much earlier than any of these grid plan foundations although in its rough chequer plan, in which streets and blocks follow the natural topography of the site rather than a geometrically correct shape, it may be a herald for the re-emergence of grid plans.

Economic Activity

The development of the town cannot be separated from activities within it. A review of all of these is beyond the scope of this paper, but in order to understand the growth of the town within an international framework, it is necessary to examine its commercial connections.

Although the documentary references to the overseas trade of Drogheda are sparse, it is clear that it was a predominantly Irish Sea traffic. Connections with Flanders and Gascony were well established and there is also evidence demonstrating contact further afield with the Hansa towns, such as Gdansk,[214] and with Iceland[215] to the north and Spain and Portugal on the south.[216] However there is as yet no good indicator of how strong these connections were. The sources are not complete enough to discern changes in the patterns of trade contact between 1200 and 1500 although it is to be expected that archaeological excavations might uncover such evidence. It is probable for instance that trade with Iceland and Portugal only began in the fifteenth century whereas the sources demonstrate that the ports of Bristol, Chester and Bordeaux maintained strong commercial contact with Drogheda throughout the period.[217]

Wine was the major import of medieval Drogheda. It came principally from the royal dependencies of Anjou, Aquitaine and Gascony, but also during the late fourteenth century and afterwards from Spain.[218] Once landed in the town, gauged[219] and the prise taken, it was sold by the Drogheda merchants to, among others, the justiciar's forces[220] and was used in one instance to supply the royal castles of Rindown and Roscommon.[221] Merchants, nobles and churchmen needed wine and it was to be found in many private cellars and in the inns.[222] Apart from supplying local and regional needs the wine was occasionally shipped out to Ulster or Scotland.[223] Most of the wine was carried by Drogheda merchants, but English and French merchants (from Bordeaux and Brittany) were also active.[224] There are a number of instances in which Chester merchants sent vessels to Bordeaux and brought the wines back to Chester via Drogheda.[225] Drogheda vessels were themselves occasionally chartered to bring wines direct from Bordeaux to Chester.[226] Iron and salt were also imported[227] and the instances of repeated horse-shoeing at Drogheda suggest that much of the iron was of poor quality.[228]

The organisation of shipping is in itself interesting. It is evident that there was a contract between the merchant and the ship-owner, master and steersman, and that their functions were distinct.[229] The merchant hired a vessel, and the owner employed a master and steersman. Goods such as hides or corn were usually carried on the outward journey and sold at a suitable port of call. Wines were then loaded for the homeward crossing.[230] The hazards of wind and weather sometimes made it impossible to return to the home port and vessels were frequently blown off course. The "La Magdeleyne" of Drogheda returning from Bordeaux in 1340 was driven by a storm to Galway.[231] Piracy was a constant danger. The Scots seem to have been particularly active in the north Irish Sea, capturing vessels and holding merchants for ransom.[232] Spanish and Breton pirates also preyed on Drogheda ships.[233]

The major export was agricultural produce. It was wheat that William Symcock shipped to Bordeaux in 1412 in order to bring back wines.[234] At the close of the thirteenth century the royal armies of Scotland, Wales and Gascony were supplied with wheat, oats, flour and and victuals from Drogheda.[235] Interestingly, it was the same merchant Hugh Morice who received each of these commissions.[236] Corn and victuals were regularly shipped to England and especially to Chester.[237] William Symcock was also involved in the transportation of victuals to Scotland in 1375.[238] Hides were exported and there is evidence that they were traded with Southampton, Dieppe and in Flanders.[239] During the fifteenth century fish was exported and salmon, presumably from the Boyne, was being sent to Chester in 1477-78.[240] Animals on the hoof were shipped out but there are no indications that this was very regular.[240] Wool was also exported from the town.[242]

Drogheda was the centre of a sizable Irish trade. The connections with Ulster and Roscommon have already been noted, and wine and corn were shipped to Waterford, Cork, Kilkenny, Wexford, Kinsale and Youghal.[243] The town acted as a market place for much of the surrounding countryside and goods were carried in small barges up the Boyne as far as Trim.[244] The murage grants indicate that oxen, horses, sheep, pigs, wheat, rye, barley, oats, butter, cheese, apples, salmon, eels and seafish were marketed in the town.[245]

The town was not just a market place, but also an industrial centre and the home of specialist craftsmen. The royal commands to construct galleys[246] indicate that it was an important ship-building centre and the murage grant of 1296 to Drogheda in Meath, in which large boards, masts, rigging ropes and canvas for ships were subject to tax, suggests that the building yards may have been on the south side.[247] That cloth was manufactured is evident from the entry in the pipe roll of 6 Edw III (1332-3) in which a cloth of divers colours, made by John son of Walter Jordan of Drogheda, was purchased to cover both exchequers of the king at Dublin.[248] Dyer Street, located close to the Boyne, was an area of woollen manufacturing.[249] The *vico furni* mentioned c. 1230 probably functioned for a time as a potters' or bakers' quarter; its whereabouts is now unknown.[250] Both wind and water power were harnessed by the millers. There was a mill beside the bridge,[251] while in 1381 a licence was issued to convert the keep of the motte atop the eponymous Millmount into a mill.[252] Building and construction work can be attested all through the period, and since the houses were both of stone and timber the skills of masons and carpenters were required. Drogheda craftsmen, for instance, worked on the castles of Dundrum, Greencastle (Co. Down), Newcastle McKinegan and Roscommon.[253] Hugh the mason was living in Drogheda during the first half of the thirteenth century[254] while the barbican of St. Laurence's Gate may have been built by William of Drogheda, the mason who worked for Edward I at Harlech in Wales.[255] Other occupations for which there is evidence include metal-workers, leather-workers,skinners and butchers.[256] The inns seem to have acted not only as places for refreshment but also as livery stables.[257] The employment of numbers of men in the haulage and loading of goods in the dock area is to be assumed. Fishing also seems to have been a full-time occupation for some.[258] An early fourteenth century poem indicates that Drogheda was also a centre for rope making, perhaps for ships.[259]

The size of Drogheda's population prior to 1349 remains a matter of speculation. J.C. Russell, the historical demographer, suggested 3,000 and more recently Brian Graham has estimated that it lay between 1000-2000.[260] Russell's own average density of 100-120 people per hectare however would put the population closer to 5,000.[261] On the other hand an estimate based on burgage holdings, with the total burgage rent at £66.13.4 and a value of 1s per plot, comes to 1333 and multiplying this by Graham's factor of five[262] one arrives at a population of about 6,600.

Potential for future research

Of the aspects not treated in this paper, municipal organisation has already been examined by Gearóid MacNiocaill,[263] but an assessment is needed of political life within the town and the town's role as a political force in medieval Ireland. Apart from the suggested anti-Geraldine stance of the town in the mid-fifteenth century, little is known of the latter. Religious life within the town has been partially looked at by Gwynn[264] but there is much still untapped in the Armagh registers. The picture of the life of the individual emerges only from court cases and the occasional walls;[265] there are sufficient references relating to the activities of some of the great merchants such as Hugh Morice and William Symcock for them to take shape before our eyes.

For topographical research the major potential source is the archaeological layers beneath modern street level. At John Street for instance the presence of 1.5m of archaeological stratification has been noted.[266] There has been much disturbance within the medieval town as the accompanying figure shows, but archaeological layers would appear to be intact over 50% of the town. Indeed in many of the areas where disturbance has occurred it is unlikely that this has penetrated down to the subsoil in all instances and in any area of the town where sites become available, archaeological investigation should take place. This need not be rescue excavation for the sake of rescue excavation. It can and should be used to clear up some of the wider research problems concerning the growth and form of the medieval town.

The understanding of Drogheda's development and of life within it is important not only for urban archaeology. It is impossible to assess the settlement pattern within the region about it without a knowledge of Drogheda's role. Excavation within the town should consider two aspects. Firstly the detailed history of a particular site, and secondly what it tells about wider developments in Drogheda and in Ireland. For the former aspect excavation within the sites of the hospitals of St. John and St.

James, about which almost nothing is known is a priority; similarly the positions of the mural towers need to be established. Housing forms within particular areas could reflect social distinctions – Dyer Street, Green Lane (formerly Irish Street), Cord Road (eastern suburb), for instance. Individual buildings such as St. Saviour's chapel and the Tholsel on the Meath side should also be examined when the opportunity arises. The nature of the port area, on the east of the bridge also needs to be determined. Excavation would also yield results on the wider problems which Drogheda shares with other west European towns, its original nucleus for instance, and should be able to determine whether the suggestion made above – that most of the town on the north side was established by 1215 - is correct or not. The analysis of pottery and other objects should be able to determine the shifts in trading contact. The profusion of new buildings, especially church towers, in the fifteenth century and the extended contacts with Portugal and Iceland suggest that this was a time of prosperity for the town; as yet this remains simply a suggestion, but excavation could determine its accuracy. Excavation is sometimes costly and its expenses can only be met from State or Corporation funds, yet Drogheda's past is as important as York's, Winchester's, or for that matter Novgorod's, and it requires examination now before it is too late.

Acknowledgments

I would like to thank Tim O'Neill f.s.c. for discussing fourteenth and fifteenth century trade with me and for giving me many references thereto; Edward Bourke for his help with the drawings and Noel Ross for his patience and support in seeing this paper through. For affording me assistance and facilities I would like to thank Moira Corcoran and Prof. George Eogan.

Bathe House: see figure 3.
This building was erected in Drogheda by Nicholas Bathe, of a Norman family, one of whom had been mayor of Drogheda in 1356. It occupied the junction of Laurence Street and Shop Street and was composed chiefly of oak obtained from Mellifont Park, Tullyallen. It was three storeys high. On the bressummer in Laurence Street was the following inscription in raised letters
"Made by Nicholas Bathe in the ieare of ovr Lord God 1570 bi hiv Mor Carpenter."
The oak beam on which the inscription was made is now preserved in the National Museum.

Drogheda Street Names

Modern	Medieval	Date	Source
Bachelors Lane	Upper lane to Friars Minor	1313	*Gormanston Reg.*, 65
	Seinte Lenes lane	1323	*ibid.*, 71
	Lane to St. Elena's well	1335	*ibid.*, 78
Bessexwell Lane	Lane to Friars minor	1320	*ibid.*, 64
Curry's Hill	? street to Carmelite Friars	1363	*ibid.*, 78
Dyer Street	Dyer strete	1329	*ibid.*, 75
Fair Street	Feyrstret	1358	*Dowdall Deeds*, no. 214
Freeschool Lane	Frumboldeslane	1436	*Swayne Reg.*, 165
Green Lane	Irish Street (*vicus Hibernicorum*)	1312	*Gormanston Reg.*, 63
James Street	St. James' Street	1467-8	Berry, *Statutes...* 1-12 *Edw IV*, 643
John Street	Road near the Castle	c.1250	*Reg. John the Baptist Dublin no.* 234
	St. John Street	1317	*ibid.*, no. 235
Laurence Street	East Street	c. 1250	*ibid.*, no 237
	St. Laurence Street	1351	*Gormanston Reg.*, 77
Magdalene Street	Road to the north gate	c. 1250	*Reg: John the Baptist Dublin* no. 237
Oulster Lane	Lyderwederlane	1314	*Gormanston Reg.*, 62
Peter Street	Great North Street	1331	*ibid.*, 74
	St. Peter's Street	1351	*ibid.*, 70
Rope Walk	Street to the Friars Preachers	1341	*ibid.*, 75
Shop Street	Bodestrata	c. 1214	C.L.A.J., XIV., 3, (1959), 158
	Bothe Street	c. 1294	*Llanthony Cartularies*, 140
Stockwells Lane	Rochstrete	1407	*Dowdall Deeds* no. 369
West Street	street to the West Gate	1247-156	*Llanthony Cartularies*, 106
	Great West Street	1323	*Gormanston Reg.*, 71
William Street	Wynhalyzereslane	1343	*ibid.*, 65
	Wynhalierlane	1436	*Swayne Reg.*, 165

FOOTNOTES:

1   *A view of Drogheda from Balls Grove* and *A view of Drogheda* which at present hang in Drogheda Public Library and are on loan from Drogheda Corporation. The pictures are not mentioned by Strickland but receive passing notice in Anne Crookshank and the Knight of Glin. *The Painters of Ireland 1660-1860* (London. 1978) 64. See *Irish Houses and Landscapes* (Exhibition Catalogue, Dublin - Belfast, 1963), nos. 38-39

2   H.J. Lawlor, "A Calendar of the Register of Archbishop Sweteman," *Proc. Roy. Ir. Acad.* 29C, (1911-12), 213-310; the entries relating to Co. Louth were published by Gwynn in *C.L.A.J.*, XI, 3, (1947), 187-203. H.J. Lawlor, "A Calendar of the Register of Archbishop Fleming," *Proc. Roy. Ir. Acad.,* 30C, (1912-13), 94-190; the entries relating to Co. Louth were published by Gwynn in *C.L.A.J.*, XI, 4, (1948), 221-237.

   D.A. Chart (ed.), *The Register of John Swayne* (Belfast, 1935), W.G.H. Quigley and E.F.D. Roberts, *Registrum Iohannis Mey* (Belfast, 1972).

   L.P. Murray (continued by Aubrey Gwynn), "Archbishop Cromer's Register," *C.L.A.J.,* VII, 4, (1932), 516-24; VIII, 1, (1933) 38-49; VIII, 2, (1934), 169-88; VIII, 3, (1935), 257-74; VIII, 4, (1936), 322-51; IX, 1, (1937) 36-41; IX, 2, (1938), 124-30; X, 2, (1942), 116-27; X, 3, (1943), 165-79.

   L.P. Murray, "A Calendar of the Register of Primate George Dowdall," *C.L.A.J.,* V1, 2, (1926), 90-100; V1, 3, (1927), 147-58; VI, 4 (1928), 213-28; VII, 1 (1929), 78-95; VII, 2, (1930), 258-75.

   The Registers of Primates Prene and Octavian have not been published.

3   E. St. John Brooks (ed.), *The Irish Cartularies of Llanthony Prima & Secunda* (Dublin, 1953); E. St. John Brooks (ed.). *Register of the Hospital of St. John the Baptist, Dublin* (Dublin 1936); Charles McNeill (ed.), *Registrum de Kilmainham* (Dublin, n.d.); "Calendar to Christ Church Deeds" in Appendix to the 20th, 23rd, 24th and 27th *Report of the Deputy Keeper of the Public Records in Ireland* (Dublin, 1888, 1891, 1892, 1896); James Mills (ed.), *Account Roll of the Priory of the Holy Trinity Dublin 1337-1346* (Dublin, 1891); J. T. Gilbert (ed.), *Chartularies of St. Mary's Abbey, Dublin,* 2 vols Rolls Series (London, 1884); J.T. Gilbert (ed.). *Register of the Abbey of St. Thomas, Dublin,* Rolls Series (London, 1889); M.V. Clarke (ed.) *Register of... Tristernagh* (Dublin, 1941); Fr. Colmcille, "Seven Documents from the old Abbey of Mellifont," *C.L.A.J.,* XIII, 1, (1953) 35-67. "An Important Mellifont Document", *ibid.,* XIV, 1, (1957), 1-13; Newport B. White, *Extents of Irish Monastic Possessions, 1540-41* (Dublin, 1943).

4   J. Mills and M. J. McEnery (eds.), *Calendar of the Gormanston Register* (Dublin, 1916).

5   Charles McNeill and A.J. Otway-Ruthven (eds.), *Dowdall Deeds* (Dublin 1960).

6   H.S. Sweetman, *Calendar of Documents relating to Ireland 1171-1307,* 5 vols (London, 1875-86); J. Mills (ed.), *Calendar of the Justiciary Rolls... of Ireland 23-35 Edw I* (Dublin, 1905, 1914); H. Wood, A.E. Langman and M.C. Griffith (eds.), *Calendar of the Justiciary Rolls... of Ireland 1-7 Edw II* (Dublin, n.d.); H.F. Berry (ed.), *Statutes and Ordinances and Acts of the Parliament of Ireland – King John to Henry V* (Dublin, 1907); H.F. Berry (ed.) *Statute Rolls of the Parliament of Ireland - King John to Henry V* (Dublin, 1907); H.F. Berry (ed.), *Statute Rolls of the Parliament of Ireland, King Henry VI* (Dublin, 1910); H.F. Berry (ed.) *Statute Rolls of the Parliament of Ireland, 1-12 Edward IV* (Dublin, 1914); J.F. Morrissey (ed.) *Statute Rolls of the Parliament of Ireland 12/13-21/22 Edward IV* (Dublin, 1939); Edward Tresham, *Rotulorum Patentium et Clausorum Cancellariae Hiberniae Calendrium Hen II - Hen VII* (Dublin, 1828); *Chartae Priviligiae et Immunitates* (Irish Record Commission, 1829); J.T. Gilbert, *Historic and Municipal Documents of Ireland 1170-1320* Rolls Series (London, 1870); *Calendar of Patent Rolls Edward II - Henry VII* 45 vols. (London, 1891-1916); *Calendar of Close Rolls Edward II - Henry VII* 41 vols. (London, 1892-1963); O. Davies and D.B. Quinn (eds.), *The Irish Pipe Roll of 14 John 1211-1212* Supplement to the *Ulster Journal of Archaeology,* 4, (1941); James Graves (ed.), *Roll of Proceedings of King's Council in Ireland 1392-1393* Rolls Series (London, 1877); M.J. McEnery (ed.) "Accounts of the Great Rolls of the Pipe of the Irish Exchequer 13 Hen III-22 Edw III" in Appendices to the 35-39th, 42-45th, 47th, 53-54th *Reports of the Deputy Keeper of the Public Records of Ireland* (Dublin, 1903-07, 1911-13, 1915, 1926-7).

7   Gearóid Mac Niocaill, *Na Buirgéisí XII-XV aois,* 1 vol. in 2, (Dublin, 1964).

8   Diarmuid Mac Iomhair, "Two Old Drogheda Chronicles," *C.L.A.J.,* XV, 1, (1961), 88-95.

9   Thomas Gogarty, *Council Book of the Corporation of Drogheda 1649-1734* (Drogheda, 1915). L.P. Murray, "Old Title Deeds of Co. Louth," *C.L.A.J.,* VII, 2, (1930), 168-173; VII, 3, (1931), 402-6; VII, 4, (1932), 488-95; VIII, 1, (1933), 52-60; VIII, 2, 193-209; VIII, 3, (1935), 283-8; X, 1, (1941), 63-6. K.W. Nicholls, "A Calendar of Salved Chancery Pleadings concerning County Louth," *C.L.A.J.,* XVII, 4, (1972), 250-60; XVIII, 2, (1974),

112-120. Diarmuid MacIomhair, "Some Drogheda Documents," *C.L.A.J.*, XVIII 1, (1973), 1-6. J. Deane, "Extracts from Isaac Butler's Journal," *C.L.A.J.*, V, 2, (1922), 93-108; see also *Jrl. of Association for the Preservation of the Memorials of the Dead, Ireland*. II, no. 1, (1892), 161-3.

10   John D'Alton, *The History of Drogheda*, 2 vols. (Dublin, 1844).

11   W.P. Allen, "Some Notes on the Old Fortifications of Drogheda," *C.L.A.J.*, X, 3, (1943), 233-44; Matthew J. Kelly, "Two Castles of Drogheda," *C.L.A.J.*, IX, 3 (1939), 244-5; "Three Monasteries of Drogheda," *C.L.A.J.*, X, 1, (1941), 25-41; 'Some Wooden Houses of Drogheda," *C.L.A.J.*, X, 1, (1941), 67-9; "The Church of St. Saviour's, Drogheda, *C.L.A.J.*, IX, 4, (1940), 346-51; Maurice P. Sheehy, "A Medieval Foundation in the Borough of Drogheda in Oirghialla," *C.L.A.J.*, XIV, 3, (1959), 154-9; Moira Corcoran, "A Drogheda Census List of 1798," *C.L.A.J.*, XVII, 2, (1970), 91-6; "The Streets and Lanes of Drogheda, 1 – Medieval," *Journal of the Old Drogheda Society*, No. 2, (1977), 22-30.

12   Avril Thomas, "Drogheda 1574" *C.L.A.J.*, XVIII, 3, (1975), 179-186.

13   R.A. Skelton, "Tudor town plans in John Speed's "Theatre" *Archaeological Journal*, 108, (1951), 115.

14   Stanihurst writing in 1577 described Drogheda as "the best town in Ireland, and truly not far behind some of the cities," quoted in T.W. Moody, F.X. Martin, F.J. Byrne (eds.), *A New History of Ireland III* (Oxford, 1976), 159. For an example of the process outlined, see A.R. Orme, "Youghal, Co. Cork - Growth, Decay and Resurgence," *Irish Geography*, V, No. 3 (1966), 121-149.

15   1657 – "A plot of the town of Drogheda," reproduced in D'Alton *op. cit.*, ii, facing p.285; 1744 - *Map in Tindal's Continuation of Rapin's History* reproduced in Gilbert Camblin, *The Town in Ulster* (Belfast, 1951) facing p. 40; 1749 - Map of Drogheda by Joseph Ravell, reproduced in D'Alton *op. cit.*, ii, facing p. 363.

16   John Maher, "Francis Place in Drogheda, Kilkenny and Waterford, etc." *J.R.S.A.I.*, 64, (1934), 41-53, Liam Price (ed.), *An Eighteenth Century Antiquary*, (Dublin, 1942); Francis Grose, *The Antiquities of Ireland* (London, 1791-5); R.M. Elmes and Michael Hewson, *Catalogue of Irish Topographical Prints and Original Drawings* (Dublin, 1975); L.F. Branigan, "An Old View of Drogheda," *C.L.A.J.*, VII, 3, (1931), 406; see also *C.L.A.J.*, II, 2, (1909), 170. A view of c. 1710 hangs in the entrance hall of Beaulieu House.

17   O. Davies, "Old Churches in County Louth - Drogheda Barony" *C.L.A.J.*, XI, 1, (1945), 21-7.

18   O. Davies, *op. cit.*, 22-3.

19   Lord Walter FitzGerald, "St. Peter's Parish - Drogheda," *Jrl. Assoc. Mem. Dead Irl.*, IV, no. i, (1898), 273-9; John Hunt, "Carved Stones, St. Peter's Church, Drogheda," *C.L.A.J.*, XIII, 1, (1953), 34; H.M. Roe, *JRSAI*, 99, (1969), 15. Portion of an Elcock mantlepiece lies against the north wall of St. Peter's, see *C.L.A.J.* X, 3, (1943), frontispiece and 216-9; it was moved here for safety by the Old Drogheda Society c. 1966.

20   The tile is similar to that reproduced by Frazer in *JRSAI*, 23, (1893), Pl. II, fig. 9, following p.358 and described on p. 363. Other examples are known from St. Patrick's and Christ Church Cathedrals, Dublin and St. Canice's Cathedral, Kilkenny. The medallion is mentioned in J.B. Leslie, *Armagh Clergy and Parishes* (Dundalk, 1911), 245.

21   "Tiles from the Old Dominican Friary, Drogheda," *C.L.A.J.*, XII, 2, (1950), 182; E. Rynne, "A Burial near the Magdalen Tower, Drogheda," *C.L.A.J.*, XIV, 3, (1959), 191.

22   Helen M. Roe, "Two Decorated Fonts in Drogheda, Co. Louth," *C.L.A.J.*, XVIII, 4, (1976), 255-62.

23   H.G. Tempest, "Two Armorial stones from Drogheda," *C.L.A.J.*, XI, 4, (1948), 252-3.

24   British Museum Reg. 1854.7.14. nos. 139-140; 1855. 12.20. nos. 20-23; 26; 1868.7.9. no. 27; 1855.12.20. no. 20 is published in G. Eogan, *Catalogue of Irish Bronze Swords* (Dublin, 1965), 73 no. 214; Greenwell Collection 1538, published in P. Harbison, *The Axes of the Early Bronze Age in Ireland* (München, 1969) no. 1693.

25   Published in Harbison, *op. cit.*, Nos. 561, 1288.

26   *Journal of the British Archaeological Association*, III, (1848), 334.

27   *ibid.*

28   R.H. M. Dolley, *The Hiberno – Norse Coins in the British Museum*, (London, 1966), 26-7; see *Clogher Record*, VII, 2, (1970), 206-7.

29   National Museum of Ireland Reg. Nos. 1976: 151-516; 518-531; 1977: 1231-2089; 1979: 91-93. There are also some finds from the Drogheda vicinity in the Royal Ontario Museum, Toronto, see *JRSAI*, 106, (1976), 73-

91, nos. 8, 25, 39, 43, 59, 78.

30   The arguments are summarised in M.M. Postan, *The Medieval Economy and Society* (Harmondsworth, 1975).

31   A.L. Mongait, *Archaeology in the U.S.S.R.* (Harmondsworth, 1961), 283-307; Fritz Rörig, *The Medieval Town* (London, 1967); Maurice Beresford, *New Towns of the Middle Ages* (London, 1967).

32   G.H. Orpen, *Ireland under the Normans*, 4 vols. (Oxford, 1911-20).

33   Brian J. Graham, "Anglo-Norman Settlement in Co. Meath." *Proc. Roy. Ir. Acad.* 75C, (1975), 223-248.

34   G. MacNiocaill, *op. cit.*

35   Gilbert, *Historic and Municipal Documents*, 3-48; see A.J. Otway-Ruthven, "The character of Norman settlement in Ireland", *Historical Studies,* V. ed. J.L. McCracken (London, 1965), 75-84.

36   *Annals of Ulster*, ii, ed. B. MacCarthy (Dublin, 1893), 130-1; see also *Annals of... the Four Masters*, i, ed. J. O'Donovan (Dublin, 1851), 1043, sub anno 1133, note e; also Gearóid Mac Niocaill, (ed.), *Notitiae as Leabhar Cheanannais 1033-1161* (Dublin, 1961), 24.

37   *C.L.A.J.,* XIII, 2 (1954), 197.

38   *C.L.A.J.,* XIII, 1, (1953), 41.

39   *ibid.* 36.

40   *Llanthony Cartularies,* 18, 100, 218.

41   Fr. Colmcille, *The Story of Mellifont* (Dublin, 1958), 295.

42   Edmund Hogan, *Onomasticon Goedelicum* (Dublin, 1910), 59.

43   Fr. Colmcille, *op. cit.,* 287.

44   *C.L.A.J.,* XIII, 2, (1954), 199.

45   *Mey Register,* 149: *Swayne Reg.,* 2.

46   *Annals of Ulster,* i. ed. B. MacCarthy (Dublin, 1887) sub annis 836, 842. The entry for 842 (recte 841) mentions a fleet at Linn Rois which O'Donovan identifies as being opposite Rosnaree, *Annals of ... the Four Masters,* i, (Dublin, 1851), sub anno 841, note q.

47   D'Alton, *op. cit.* i, 86; see F. J. Byrne, in *Proc. Roy. Ir. Acad.,* 66 C (1968), 383-400 and G. Eogan, "The Iron Age – Early Christian settlement at Knowth, Co. Meath, Ireland," in V. Markotic (ed.), *Ancient Europe and the Mediterranean: studies presented in honour of Hugh O.N. Henken* (Warminster, 1977), 68-76.

48   See notes 24-25 supra.

49   R.H. Dolley, *The Hiberno - Norse Coins in the British Museum* (London , 1966), 26.

50   Michael Herity, *Irish Passage Graves* (Dublin, 1974).

51   Orpen, *op. cit.,* ii, 79; iv, 310.

52   *Llanthony Cartularies,* 79, 302.

53   D'Alton, *op. cit.,* i, 141.

54   *Llanthony Cartularies,* 79.

55   *ibid.,* 302.

56   *ibid.,* 286; A. Gwynn and R. N. Hadcock, *Medieval Religious Houses: Ireland* (London, 1970), 189, 195.

57   MacNiocaill, *Na Buirgéisí,* i. 172-3.

58   *ibid.,* ii, 327.

59   Gormanston Reg., 66.

60   *H.E.* Salter, *Survey of Oxford*, 2 vols., Oxford Historical Society, 2nd. Ser., vols. 14, 20 (Oxford, 1956-66).

61   *Swayne Reg.,* 165.

62   D.M. Palliser, *Urban History Yearbook* 1975, 11.

63   J. Radley, in *Medieval Archaeology,* 15, (1971), 42-5.

64   *Llanthony Cartularies,* 303.

65   *Reg. John the Baptist, Dublin,* no. 234.

66   *ibid.,* no. 235.

67   *Gormanston Reg.,* pp. 78-80.

68   Gwynn and Hadcock. *op. cit.,* 211-2; White, *Extents,* 239-42.

69   D'Alton, *op. cit.,* i, 133.

70   *ibid.*

71   Morrisey, *Statute Rolls...* 12/13-21/22 *Edw. IV,* 401.

72   *JRSAI,* 64, (1934), 42.

73   Berry, *Statue Rolls...* 1-12 *Edw.* IV, 643.

74   *C.L.A.J.,* IX, 3, (1939), 245.

75   *ibid.,* Orpen, *JRSAI,* 38, (1908), 249, note 3.

76   *C.L.A.J.,* XVIII, 3, (1975), 184.

77   D'Alton, *op. cit.,* i, 135.

78   *Gormanston Reg.,* 78, 80.

79   *ibid.,* 78.

80   *Jrl. of the Old Drogheda Society,* No. 2, (1977), 27.

81   *ibid.*

82   Christ Church Deeds in *20th Report DKPRI* (1888), no. 379; *Tristernagh Reg.,* 25; White, *Extents,* 279.

83   *Llanthony Cartularies,* 218, 227.

84   D'Alton, *op. cit.,* i, 43: *C.L.A.J.,* XV, 1, (1961), 92 and 95.

85   Christ Church Deeds in *20th Report DKPRI* (1888), no. 312.

86   *Llanthony Cartularies,* 77, 302.

87   *ibid.,* 77.

88   *ibid.,* 302-3.

89   *Gormanston Reg.,* 80-81.

90   D'Alton, *op. cit.,* i, 41.

91   White, *Extents,* 247.

92   Grose, *Antiquities,* ii, pl. 47.

93   *C.L.A.J.,* XI, 1, (1945), 26.

94   *ibid.*

95   *JRSAI,* 38, (1908), 248.

96   *ibid.*

97   *Cal. Pat. Rolls* (1381-85), 49.

98   *C.L.A.J.,* V, 2, (1922), 95-6; VIII, 3, (1931), 406.

99   *C.L.A.J.,* VI, 1, (1925), facing p. 8.

100   White, *Extents,* 240, *C.L.A.J.,* X, 3, (1943), 239.

101   *Gormanston Reg.,* 69.

102   White, *Extents,* 243.

103   *C.L.A.J.,* XIV, 3, (1959), 158, incorrectly identified by Sheehy as Bodenstown, Co. Kildare; see *JRSAI* 83, (1953), 200.

104   *Llanthony Cartularies,* 140-1; *Gormanston Reg.,* 75-6.

105   *Gormanston Reg.,* 64, 66, 67, 68, 71, 75, 76.

106   Kelly, *C.L.A.J.,* IX, 4, (1940), 347; the site which he plots however is out of all proportion to the size of St. Saviour's which seems to have occupied no more than a standard burgage holding; *Llanthony Cartularies* 101-3.

107   *Llanthony Cartularies,* 102; *C.L.A.J.,* IX, 4, (1940), 348.

108   *C.L.A.J.,* IX, 4, (1940), 348.

109   *Llanthony Cartularies,* 101.

110   *ibid.*

111   *C.L.A.J.,* IX, 3, (1939), 245; *Llanthony Cartularies,* 302, *Gormanston Reg.,* 72.

112   *Llanthony Cartularies,* 302.

113   Berry, *Statutes... Hen VI,* 359, 579.

114   *Llanthony Cartularies,* 63.

115   Reg. *John the Baptist, Dublin,* no. 237.

116   *C.L.A.J.,* V, 4, (1924), 275.

117   *Gormanston Reg.,* 64, 65, 66, 72, 76, 77.

118   *ibid.,* 77.

119   *ibid.,* 81; 43 *Rep. DKPRI* (1912), 53.

120   *Reg. Mey,* 398; *Swayne Reg.* 165.

121   *Reg. Mey,* 432.

122   *ibid.*

123   *Llanthony Cartularies*, 68; *C.L.A.J.,* XIV, 3 (1959), 158.

124   *Llanthony Cartularies*, 106-7; *C.L.A.J.,* IX, 3, (1939), 244.

125   *Gormanston Reg.,* 71, 72.

126   *Dowdall Deeds,* no. 369.

127   *Swayne Reg.,* 199.

128   *ibid.;* White, *Extents,* 241.

129   *Reg. Cromer,* no. 102; *C.L.A.J.,* VIII, 3, (1935), 263.

130   *Gormanston Reg.,* 74.

131   *ibid.,* 70, 73, 74.

132   *Reg. John the Baptist, Dublin,* no. 237.

133   *Gormanston Reg.,* 75.

134   *ibid.,* 63, 75, *Jrl. Old Drogheda Society,* No. 2, (1977), 24.

135   *Gormanston Reg.,* 64, 65, 66, 71, 76, 77, 78.

136   *ibid.,* 64, 68, 69, 78; *Chartularies of St. Mary's, Dublin,* ii, 6-7.

137   *Gormanston Reg.,* 68.

138   *Gormanston Reg.,* 75.

139   *ibid.,* 70, 74; *Dowdall Deeds,* no. 214.

140   White, *Extents,* 241.

141   *Dowdall Deeds,* no. 369; see *C.L.A.J.,* VIII, 1, (1933), 54, no 3323; *Swayne Reg.* 165; *Gormanston Reg.,* 64, 65, 69.

142   *Gormanston Reg.* 77.

143   *ibid.,* 65; *Reg. John the Baptist, Dublin,* no. 237.

144   White, *Extents,* 120; *Gormanston Reg.* 70, 71.

145   *Gormanston Reg.* 66.

146   White, *Extents,* 241; *C.L.A.J.,* VII, 4, (1932), 492, no. 1761; *Llanthony Cartularies,* 105.

147   *C.L.A.J.,* XV, 1, (1961), 92, 95.

148   *Swayne Reg.,* 142.

149   *Gormanston Reg.,* 69; White, *Extents,* 248.

150   D'Alton, *op. cit.,* i, 112; White, *Extents,* 242, 246; D'Alton also mentions a St. Benet's chapel, *op. cit.,* i, 133.

151 *Llanthony Cartularies*, 18, 19-28.

152 Leslie, *Armagh Clergy and Parishes* (Dundalk, 1911), 245; Davies, C.L.A.J., XI, 1, (1945), 22.

153 C.L.A.J., V, 2, (1922), 94.

154 *Sweteman Reg.*, no. 178; *Ormond Deeds* iii, pp. 143-4; *Swayne Reg.*, 178-180; D'Alton, *op. cit.*, i, 17; Leslie *op. cit.*, 245; *C.L.A.J.*, VII, 2, (1930), 277.

155 *Swayne Reg.*, 178-80.

156 *C.L.A.J.*, XV, 1, (1961), 93.

157 *ibid.*

158 *C.L.A.J.*, XVIII, 4, (1976), 261

159 *C.L.A.J.*, XI, 1, (1945), 22.

160 *ibid.*, 23.

161 *Llanthony Cartularies*, 45.

162 Leslie, *op. cit.*, 246.

163 *Dowdall Deeds*, no. 400.

164 *Llanthony Cartularies*, 194.

165 *C.L.A.J.*, XV, 1, (1961), 93; *Llanthony Cartularies*, 19.

166 *Reg. John the Baptist, Dublin*, nos 236, 237.

167 *C.L.A.J.*, VII, 4, (1932), 491, no. 2285.

168 *C.L.A.J.*, X, 1, (1941), 37.

169 *C.L.A.J.*, VIII, 3, (1935), 277.

170 *C.L.A.J.*, X, 1, (1941), 37.

171 *ibid.*

172 E. B. FitzMaurice and A.G. Little (eds.), *Materials for the History of the Franciscan Province of Ireland A.D.*, 1230-1450 (Manchester, 1920), 132.

173 *ibid.*, 167.

174 *ibid.*, 196

175 *ibid.*, 188.

176 *ibid.*, 190; Berry, *Statutes... 1-12 Edw.* IV, 369.

177 *C.L.A.J.*, VIII, 3, (1935), 276.

178 W. Harris, *Ware's Antiquities of Ireland* (Dublin, 1762), 278; *C.D.I.* (1171-1251), 414.

179 W. Harris, *op. cit.*, 276.

180 D'Alton, *op. cit.*, i, opp. p. 120.

181 Gwynn and Hadcock, *op. cit.*, 224.

182 *Llanthony Cartularies*, 21, 63.

183 *C.L.A.J.*, XIV, 3, (1959), 191.

184 *C.L.A.J.*, XII, 2, (1950), 182.

185 Berry, *Statutes... 1-12 Edw.* IV, 613.

186 D'Alton, *op. cit.*, i, 109; *C.L.A.J.*, X, 1, (1941), 25.

187 White, *Extents*, 242, 246, 248.

188 *C.L.A.J.*, XIV, 3, (1959), 154-9.

189 *C.L.A.J.*, XI, 1, (1945), 25.

190 *C.L.A.J.*, X, 1, (1941), 31.

191 White, *Extents*, 247.

192 D'Alton, *op. cit.,* i, 116.

193 *Gormanston Reg.,* 62, 69; C.L.A.J., VII, 4, (1932), 492; *Jrl. Old Drogheda Society,* No. 2, (1977), 29; *Llanthony Cartularies,* 105.

194 *Llanthony Cartularies,* 63.

195 *Mey Reg.,* 359.

196 Illustrated in *C.L.A.J.,* XI, 1, (1945), Pl. IV, 4,5, opp. p. 25.

197 *JRSAI,* 64, (1934), Pl. VI opp. p. 43.

198 D'Alton, *op. cit.,* i, 84.

199 *Reg. John the Baptist, Dublin* 237; *Gormanston Reg.,* 71.

200 Royal Commission on Historic Monuments, *The City of York,* II: *The Defences* (London, 1972), 142-9.

201 *C.L.A.J.,* X, 3, (1943), 240.

202 *C.L.A.J.,* VII, 3, (1931), 406.

203 *Gormanston Reg.,* 64.

204 H.L. Turner, *Town Defences in England and Wales* (London, 1971), 152, 160.

205 *ibid.*

206 *C.D.I.* (1171-1251), 2135, 2614; *C.D.I.* (1252-1284), 1517; *C.D.I.* (1293-1301), 311; *Cal. Just. Rolls,* (1305-7), 336; *Cal. Pat. Rolls* (1317-21), 54; *Chartae Privilegia et Immunitates,* pp. 52, 56, 78, 82; 47 *Rep. DKPRI* (1915) 35; *Cal. Pat. Rolls* (1401-5), 419. An additional grant of 1414 is mentioned in the appendix to the *First Report of the Commissioners appointed to inquire into the Municipal Corporations in Ireland* (London, 1835-6), 807.

207 42 *Rep. DKPRI,* (1911), 48, 50; *Chartae Privilegia et Immunitates,* p. 52; *Cal. Pat. Rolls,* (1441-6), 97

208 J. Bradley, "The Town Wall of Kilkenny," *Old Kilkenny Review,* Vol. i, New Series (1974-8), 85-103, 209-218.

209 *Llanthony Cartularies,* 63.

210 *ibid.,* 105.

211 *Gormanston Reg.,* 71.

212 Some of these are discussed by Butler in M.W. Barley (ed.), *The Plans and Topography of Medieval Towns in England and Wales,* CBA Research Report No. 14 (London, 1976), 46.

213 Bradley, *op. cit.,* 87.

214 *Cal. Pat. Rolls* (1381-5), p. 501.

215 Berry, *Statutes... Hen.* VI, 697.

216 *Octavian Reg.,* TCD Ms 557/11, pp. 1097-9; *Cal. Pat. Rolls* (1354-8), 73.

217 Bristol, *C.D.I.* (1171-1251), 1875; *Cal. Pat. Rolls* (1381-5), 501; *Hist. Mss. Comm., 8th Rep.* (1881), 367-8; Chester, *C.D.I.,* (1252-84). 1718; Berry, *Statutes... Hen.* VI, 697; Bordeaux, *C.D.I.* (1252-84), 596; *C.D.I.* (1293-1301), 27; *Rot. Pat. Hib.,* 198, no. 26; see *Gormanston Reg.,* 80; 47 *Rep. DKPRI.* (1915), 65.

218 *Rot. Pat. Hib.,* 137, no. 223.

219 *C.D.I.* (1293-1301), 613.

220 *C.D.I.* (1252-84), 338, 394.

221 *C.D.I.* (1252-84), 2189; *C.D.I.,* (1285-92), 72.

222 J. Mills, *Account Roll of the Priory of the Holy Trinity, Dublin* (Dublin, 1891), 2.

223 *Rot. Pat. Hib.,* 142, no. 237; *ibid.,* 136, no. 199.

224 *C.D.I.* (1293-1301); 27; Berry, *Statutes... 1-12 Edw.* IV, 449.

225 M.K. James, *Studies in the Medieval Wine Trade,* ed. E. M. Veale (Oxford, 1971), 135, 152.

226 *ibid.,* 152; the extent of the trade between Drogheda and Chester can be seen in K.P. Wilson (ed.), *Chester Customs Accounts* 1301-1566 (The Record Society of Lancashire and Cheshire, vol. III, Liverpool, 1969.)

227 *Cal. Pat. Rolls* (1358-61), 114; *Rot. Pat. Hib.,* 257, nos. 39, 48; *ibid.,* 258-9, no. 68.

228 Mills, *op. cit.,* 2.

229 Berry, *Statutes... Hen.* VI, 291.

230   Rot. Mem. 3 Edw. II, PROI Ms. 1A/53/28 pp 425-8; RIA Ms. 12/D/12 p.84; *Rot. Pat. Hib.*, 16.

231   *Cal. Close Rolls* (1339-41), 624.

232   *Rot. Pat. Hib.*, 42, no. 17.

233   Berry, *Statutes... Hen. VI.* 601; *Statutes... 1-12 Edw.* IV, 449.

234   *Rot. Pat. Hib.*, 198, no. 26.

235   *C.D.I.* (1293-1301), 524, 368, 234.

236   *ibid.*, 217, 234, 239.

237   *C.D.I.* (1252-84), 1718; *Cal. Close Rolls* (1313-18), 396; *Cal. Close Rolls* (1374-7), 318; *Cal. Pat. Rolls* (1321-4) 217.

238   *Rot. Pat. Hib.*, 96, no. 218.

239   *Cal. Pat. Rolls* (1354-8), 73; RIA Ms. 12/D/14 p. 149; J. Mills, *Cal. Just. Rolls,* 23-31 Edw. I, 139; *Cal. Close Rolls* (1307-13), 252.

240   *Rot. Pat. Hib.*, 201, no. 110; *Hist. Mss. Comm. 8th Rep.* (1881), 367-8; K.P. Wilson (ed.), *op. cit.,* 109.

241   E.M. Carus Wilson, *Medieval Merchant Venturers* (London, 1967), 24.

242   *C.D.I.* (1252-84), 1429; Berry, *Statutes... John to Hen.* V, 315.

243   Berry, *Statutes... Hen,* VI, 171.

244   *Gormanston Reg..* 8.

245   *C.D.I.* (1171-1251), 2135; *C.D.I.* (1252-84), 1517; *C.D.I.* (1293-1301), 251, 311.

246   *C.D.I.* (1171-1251), 1049, 2532; *36 Rep. DKPRI* (1904), 24.

247   *C.D.I., (1293-1301),* 311.

248   *43 Rep. DKPRI* (1912), 53.

249   *vicus tinctorum, Gormanston Reg.,* 75.

250   *Llanthony Cartularies,* 105.

251   *C.D.I.* (1171-1251), 384.

252   *Cal. Pat. Rolls* (1381-5), 49.

253   *Reg. John the Baptist, Dublin,* 237; see Stalley in *Jrl. British Archaeol. Assoc.,* 131, (1978), 46.

254   *Llanthony Cartularies,* 246.

255   R.A. Brown, H.M. Colvin, and A.J. Taylor, *The History of the King's Works, I, The Middle Ages* (London, 1963), 1039-40.

256   *Sweteman Reg.,* no 177; Berry, *Statutes... 1-12 Edw. IV,* 563; *Cromer Reg.,* no 144 in *C.L.A.J.,* VIII, 4. (1936), 332; *Mey Reg.,* 52, 432 (goldsmithing), 65.

257   Mills, *Account Roll... Holy Trinity,* 2.

258   *Ormond Deeds,* i, no. 863.

259   W. Heuser, *Die Kildare Gedichte* (Bonn, 1904), 155; cf. St. John D. Seymour, *Anglo Irish Literature* 1200-1582 (Cambridge, 1929), 110.

260   Graham in R.A. Butlin (ed.), *The Development of the Irish Town* (London, 1977), 45; Josiah Cox Russell, *Medieval Regions and their Cities* (Newton Abbot, 1972), 137.

261   Russell, *op. cit.,* 135.

262   Graham in Butlin, *op. cit.,* 44.

263   Gearóid MacNiocaill, *Na Buirgéisí,* 1 vol. in 2; (Dublin, 1964).

264   A. Gwynn, *The Medieval Province of Armagh,* 1470-1545 (Dundalk, 1946).

265   *C.L.A.J.,* XI, 3, (1947), 199; *Swayne Reg.,* 43, 59, 90, 142.

266   R. Ó Floinn in *Excavations* 1975-76, 33.